Alabama Song 48
Back Door Man 52
Been Down So Long 16
Hello, I Love You 7
Land Ho! 40
L.A. Woman 36
Light My Fire 4
Lover Her Madly 20
Love Me Two Times 30
People Are Strange 10
Riders On The Storm 12
Strange Days 23
The Crystal Ship 34
The End 45
When The Music's Over 26
You're Lost, Little Girl 28

SUPERTAB

THE DOOORS

Wise Publications
London/New York/Sydney

Exclusive distributors:
Music Sales Limited
8/9 Frith Street, London W1V 5TZ, England.
Music Sales Pty Limited
120 Rothschild Avenue, Rosebery,
NSW2018, Australia.

This book is not authorised for sale in
the United States of America or Canada.

This book © Copyright 1989, 1995 by
Wise Publications
Order No. AM933350
ISBN 0-7119-5288-4

Unauthorised reproduction of any part
of this publication by any means
including photocopying is an
infringement of copyright.

Cover and book designed by
Pearce Marchbank Studio.
Compiled by Peter Evans.

Music Sales' complete catalogue lists
thousands of titles and is available in
full colour sections. Please state your
areas of interest and send a cheque
for £1.50 for postage to: Music Sales
Limited, Newmarket Road, Bury
St. Edmunds, Suffolk IP33 3YB.

Your Guarantee of Quality
As publishers we strive to produce
every book to the highest commercial
standards. The book has been
carefully designed to minimise awkward
page turns, and to make playing from it
a real pleasure; Particular care has been
given to specifying acid-free, neutral-sized
paper which has not been chlorine
bleached but produced with special regard
for the environment. Throughout, the printing
and binding have been planned to ensure a
sturdy, attractive publication which should
give years of enjoyment. If your copy fails
to meet our high standards, please inform
us and we will gladly replace it.

Tablature Explained

The tablature stave comprises six lines, each representing a string on the guitar as illustrated.

A number on any of the lines indicates, therefore, the string and fret on which a note should be played.

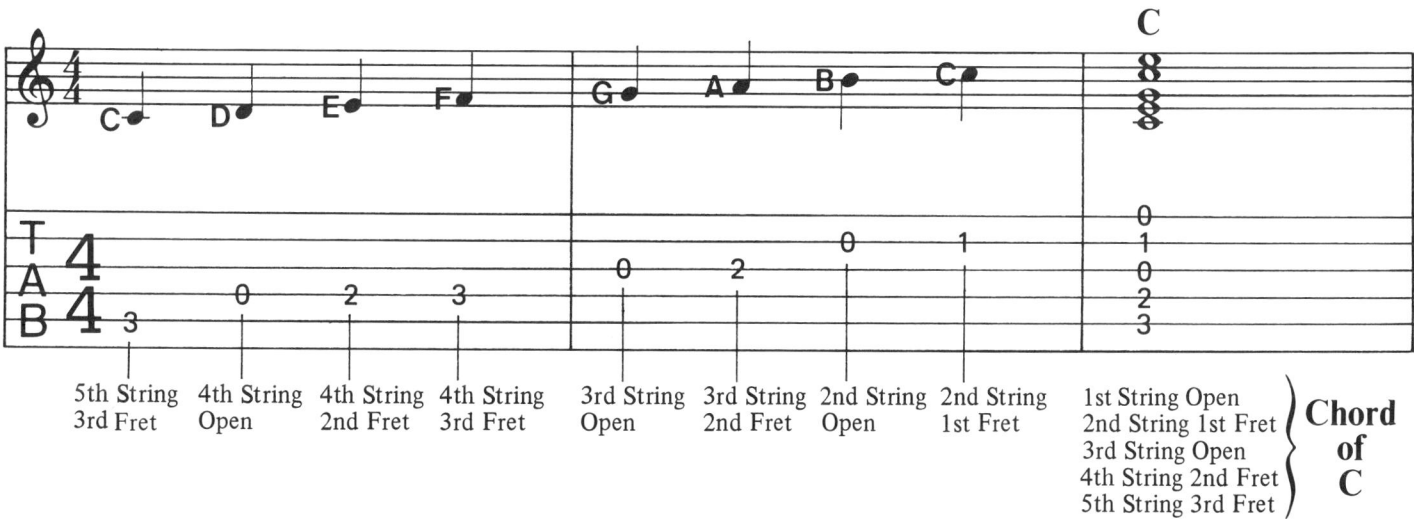

A useful hint to help you read tablature is to cut out small squares of self-adhesive paper and stick them on the neck of the guitar adjacent to each of the frets, numbering them accordingly.

Gliss (Downward)
Strike note and then slide the finger holding that note down the fretboard.

Gliss (Upward)
Same as above except slide finger up the fretboard.

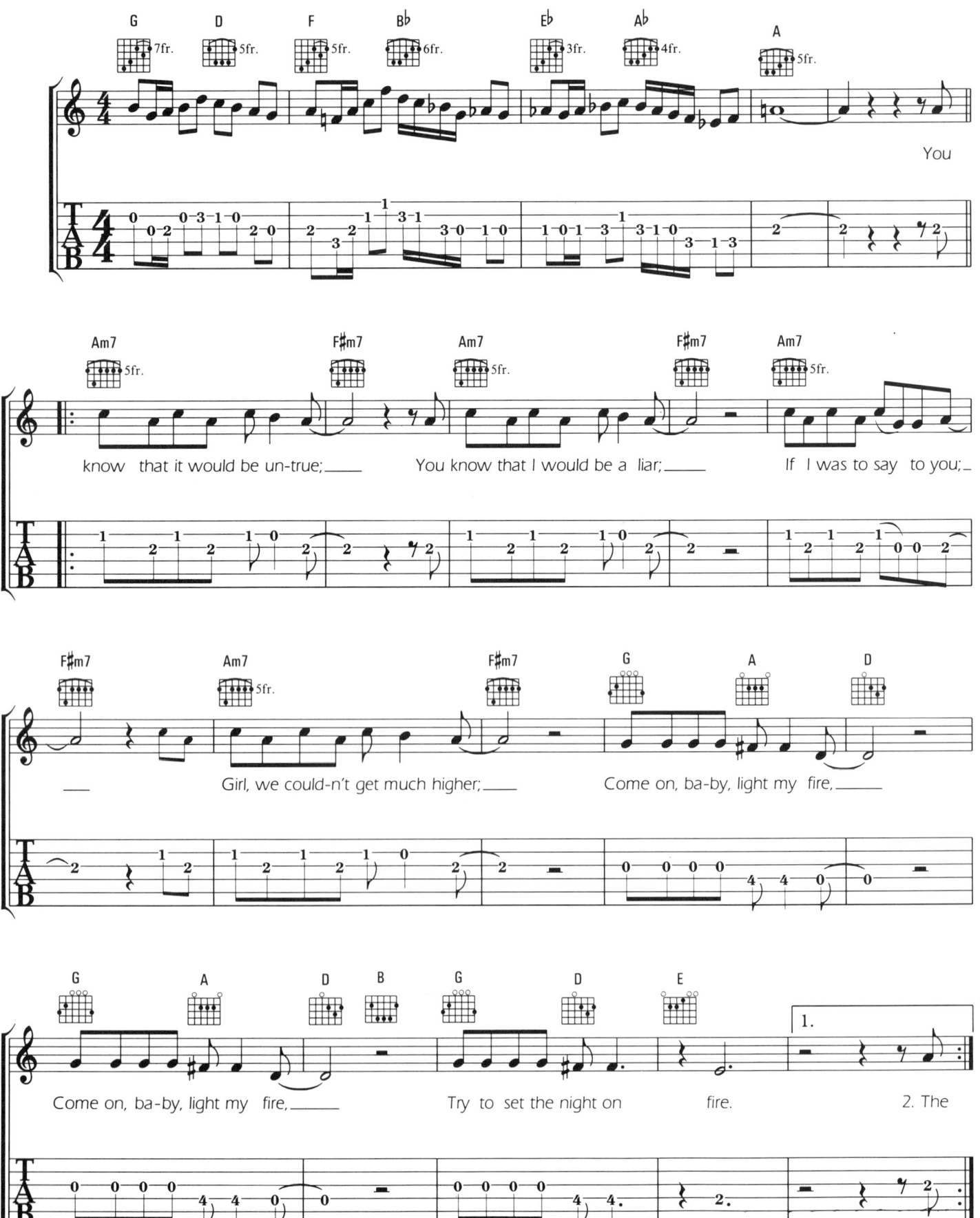

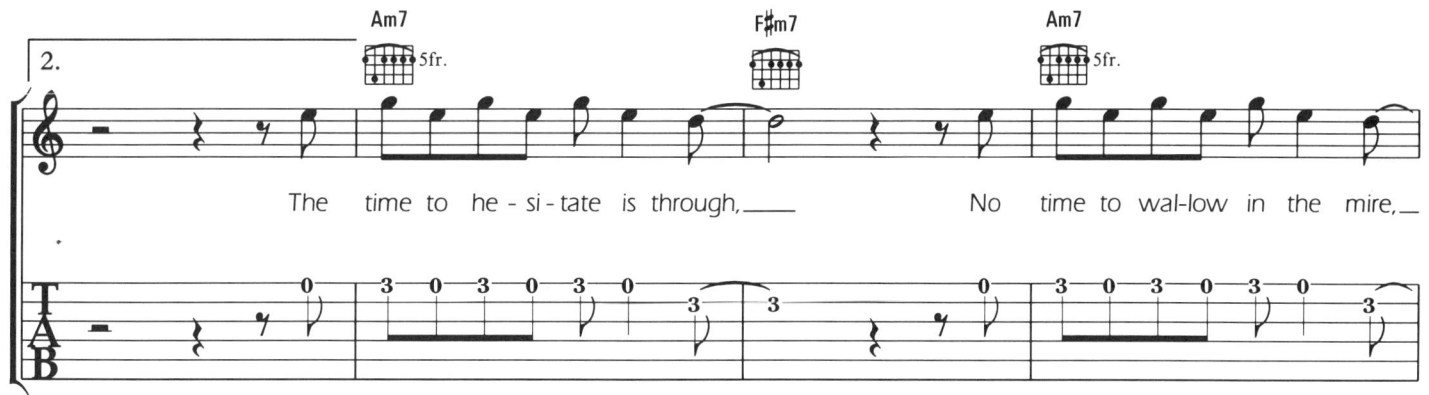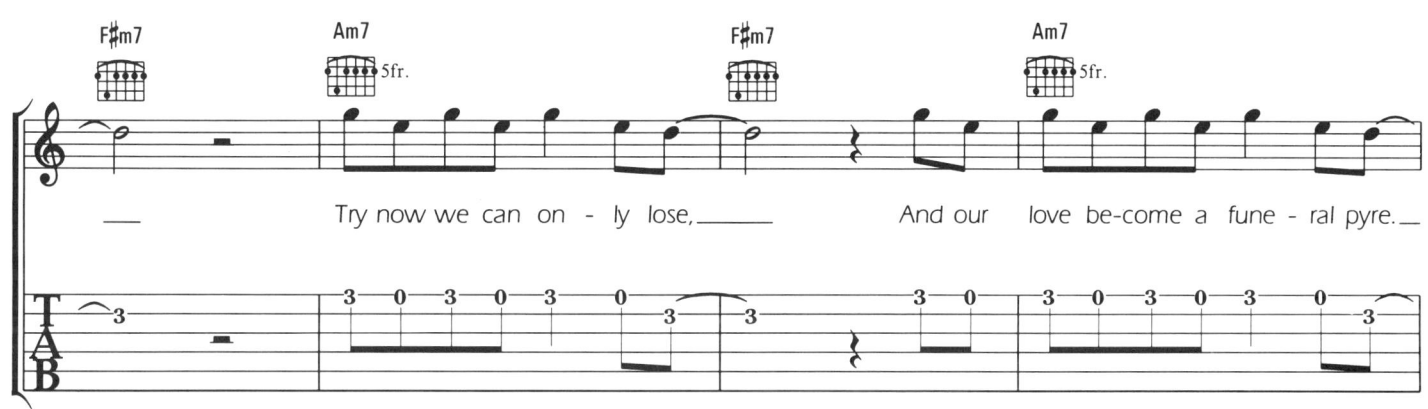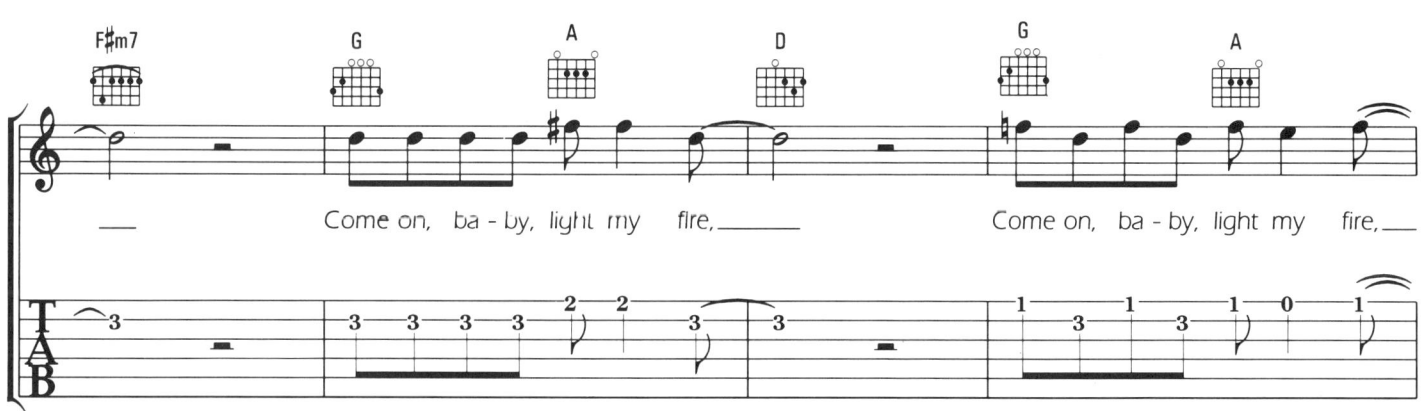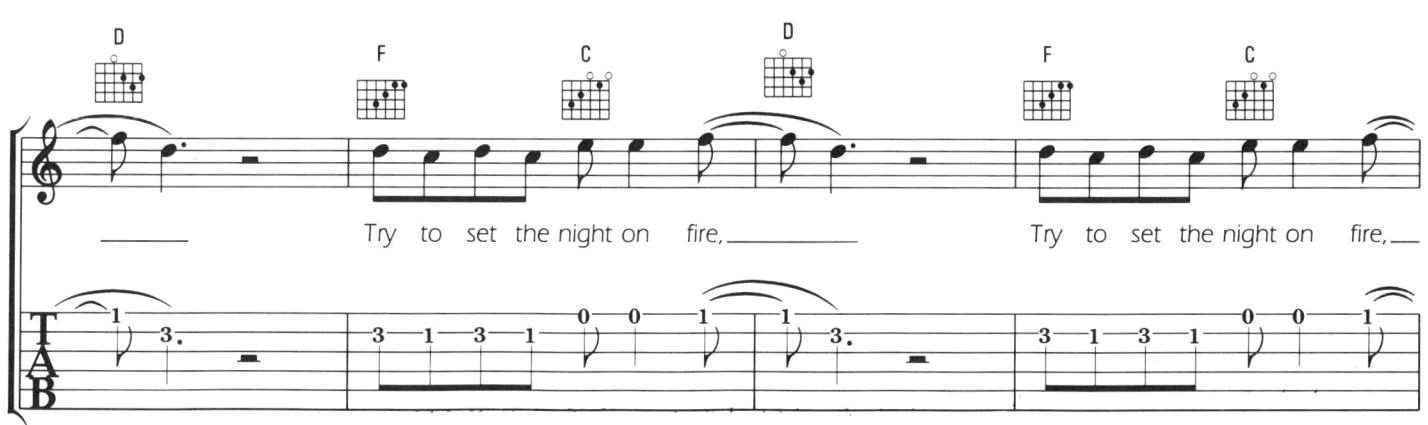

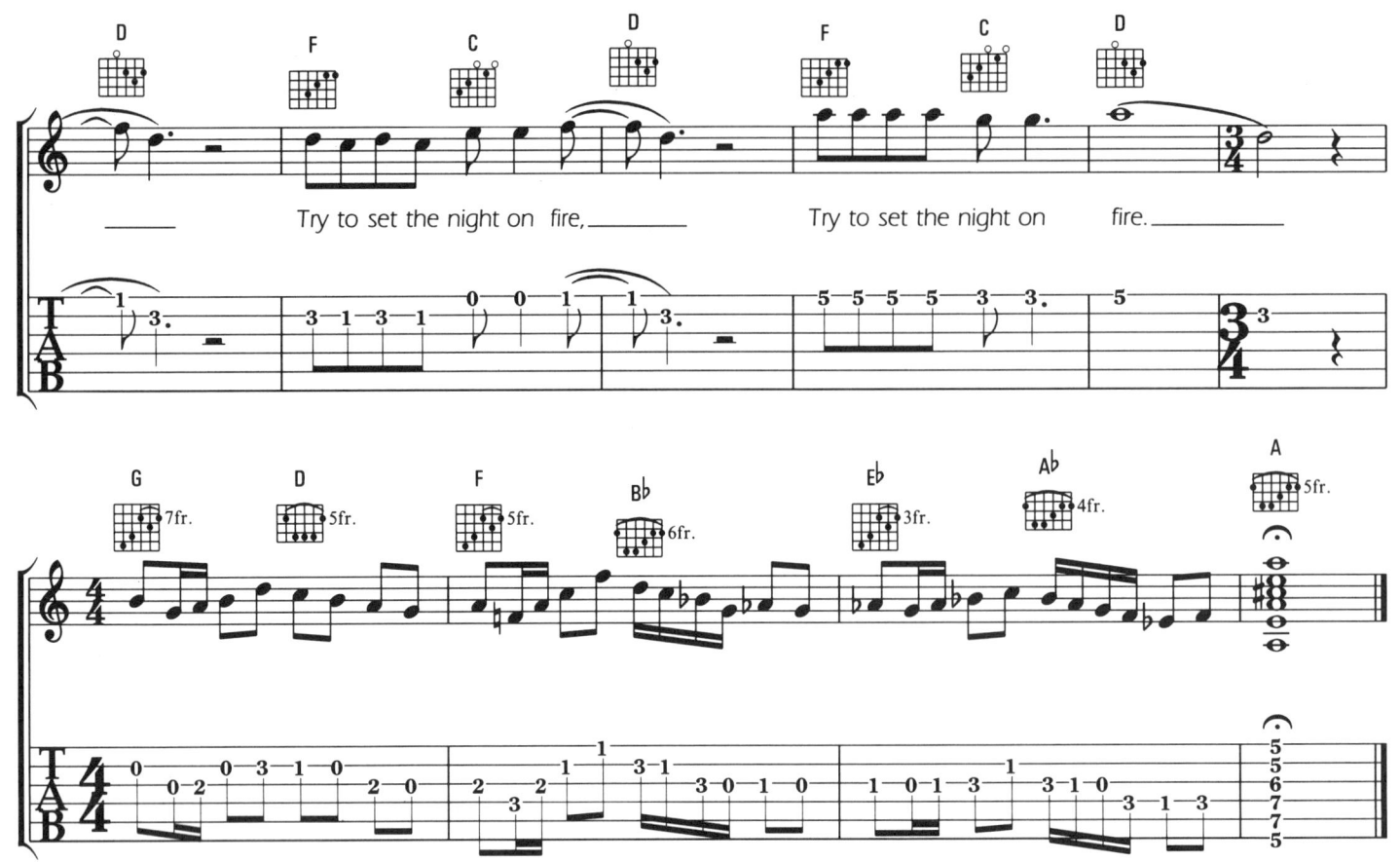

2 The time to hesitate is through,
   No time to wallow in the mire,
   Try now we can only lose,
   And our love become a funeral pyre.
   Come on, baby, light my fire,
   Come on, baby, light my fire,
   Try to set the night on fire.

HELLO, I LOVE YOU

Words & Music by The Doors

© Copyright 1968 Doors Music Company, USA. All rights for the United Kingdom, Northern Ireland & Eire controlled by Rondor Music (London) Limited, 10a Parsons Green, London SW6.
All Rights Reserved. International Copyright Secured.

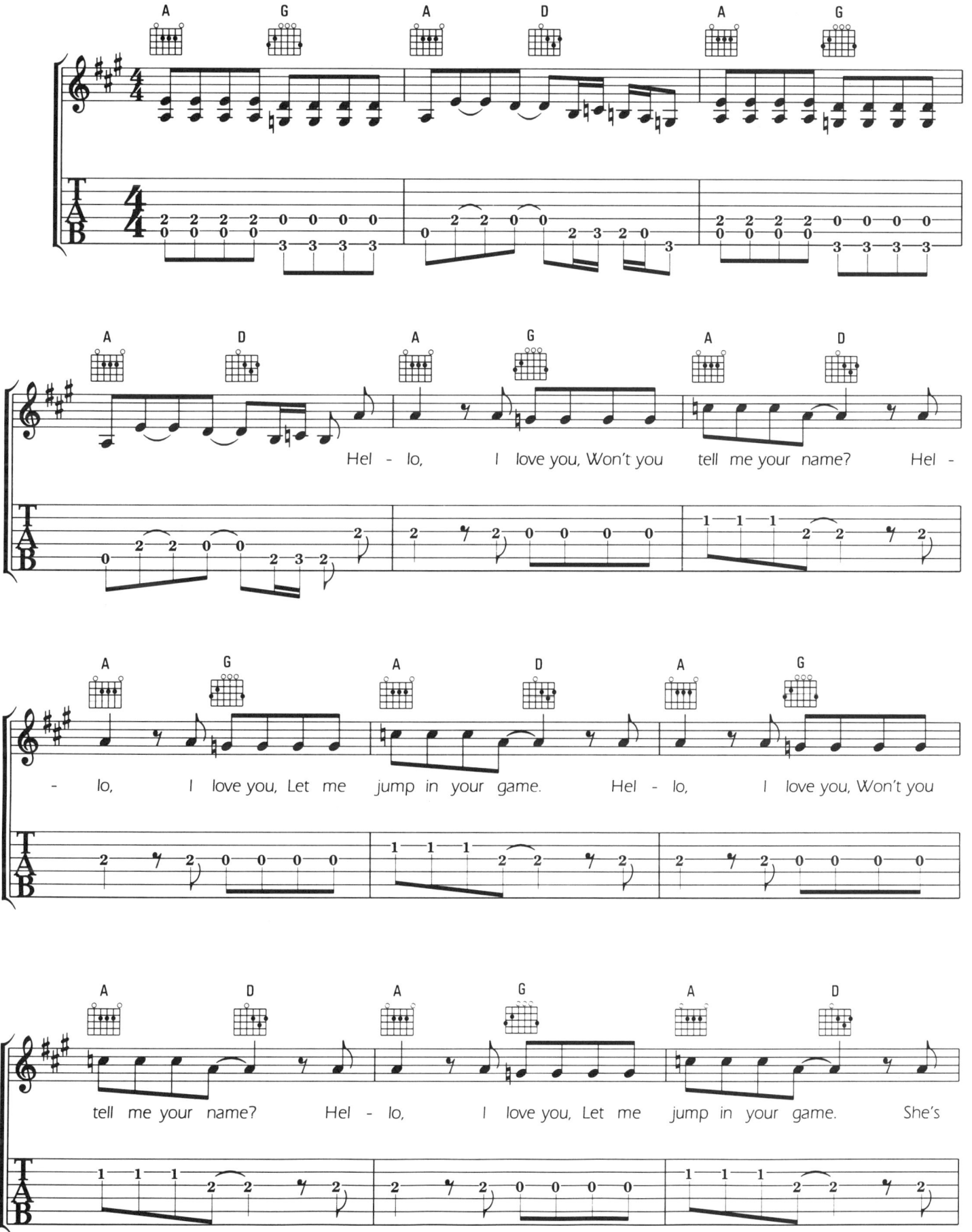

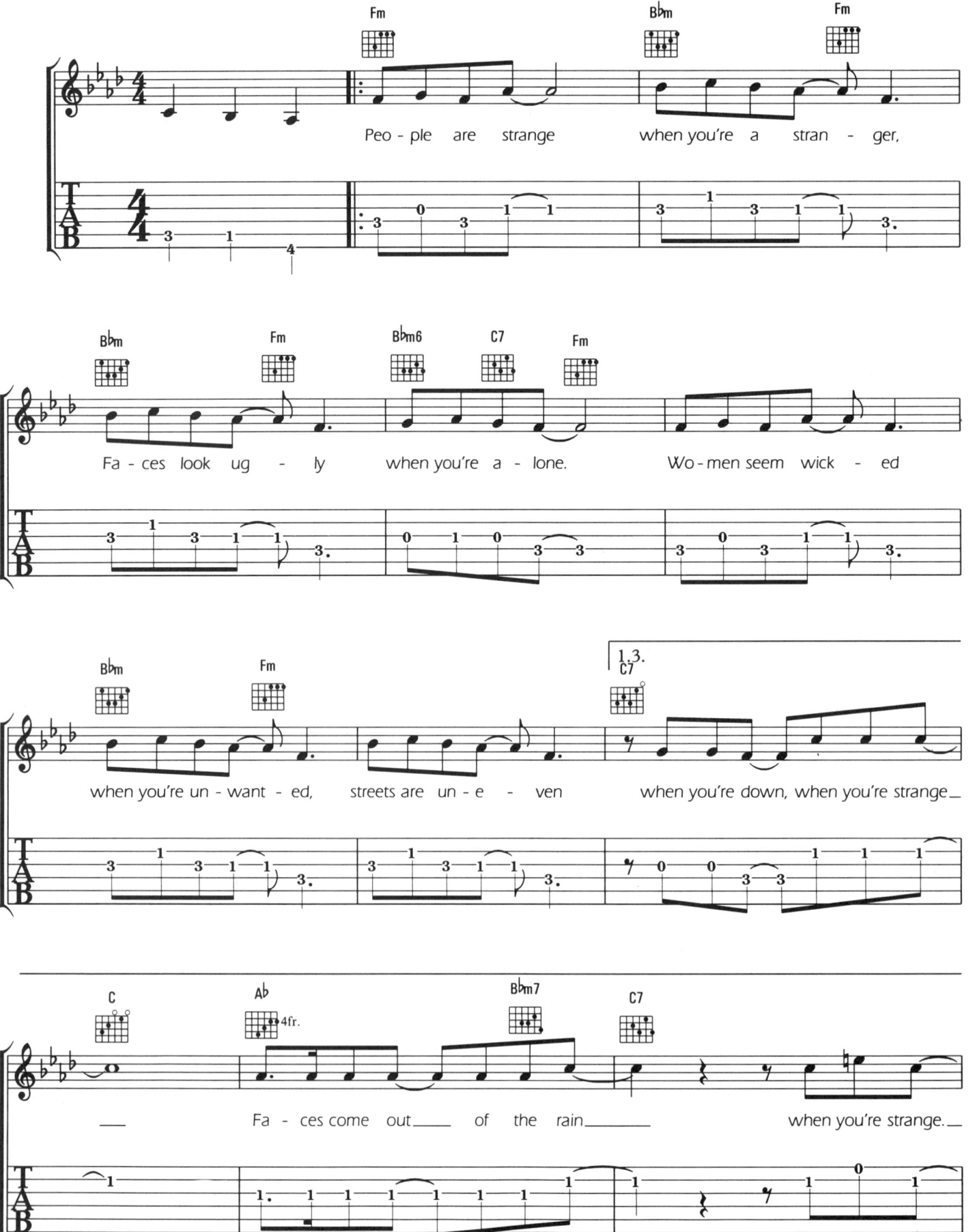

RIDERS ON THE STORM

Words & Music by The Doors

© Copyright 1971 Doors Music Company, USA. All rights for the United
Kingdom, Northern Ireland & Eire controlled by Rondor Music (London)
Limited, 10a Parsons Green, London SW6.
All Rights Reserved. International Copyright Secured.

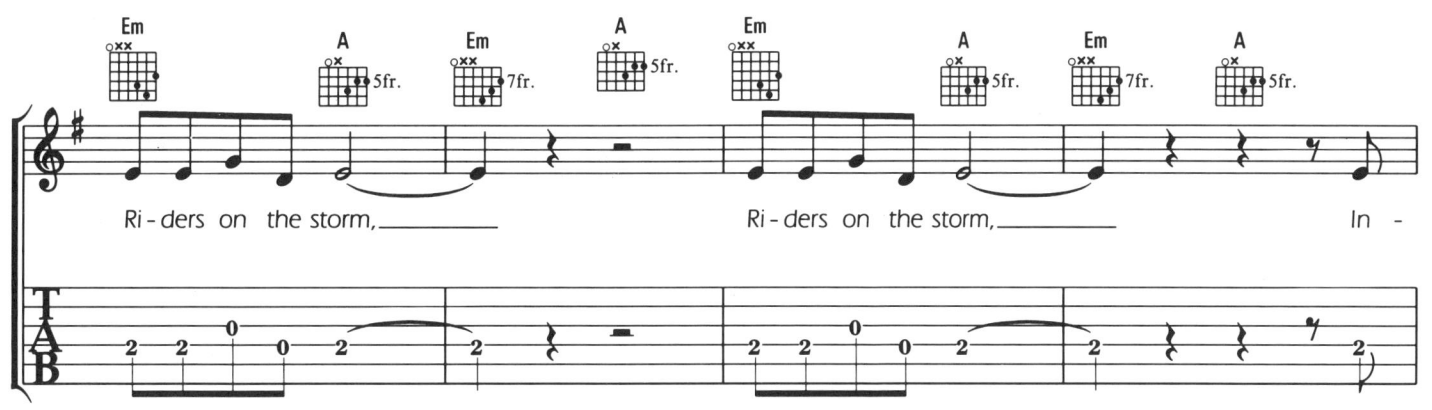
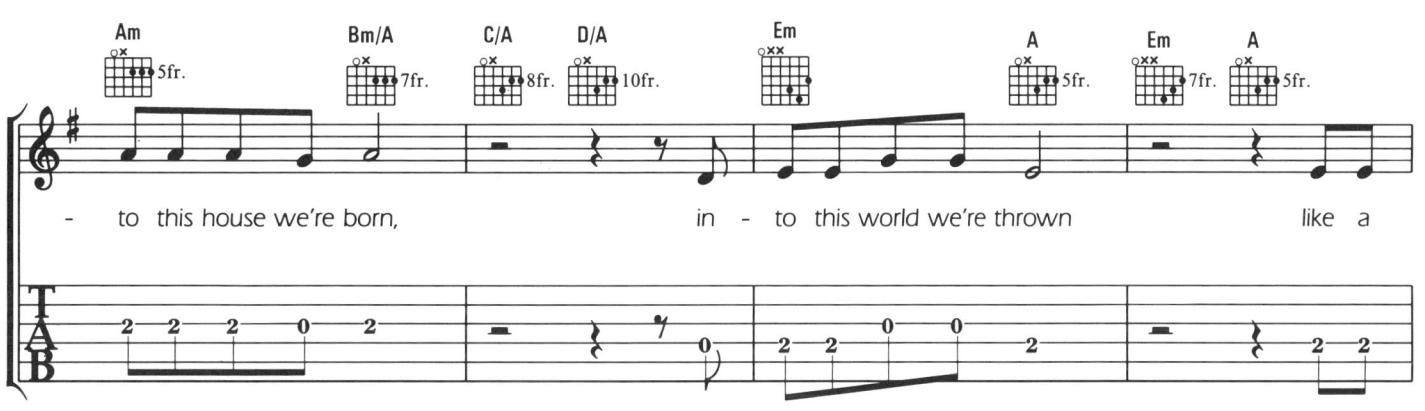
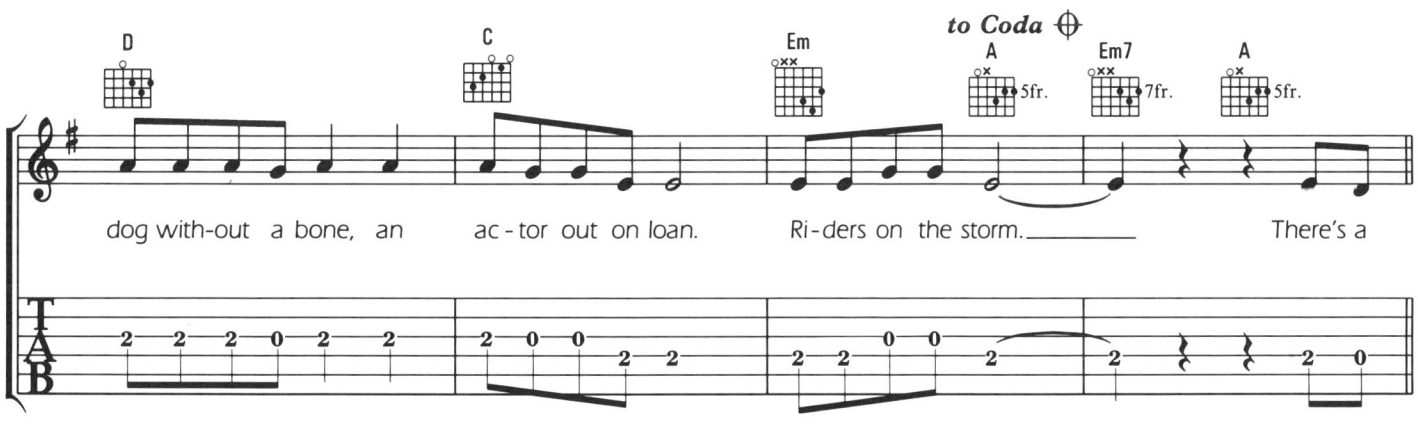
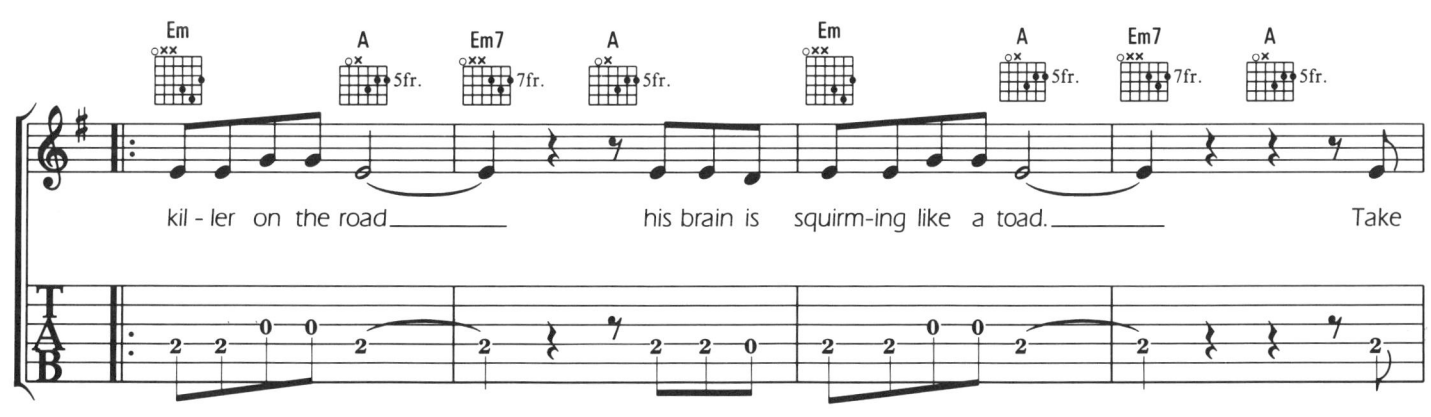

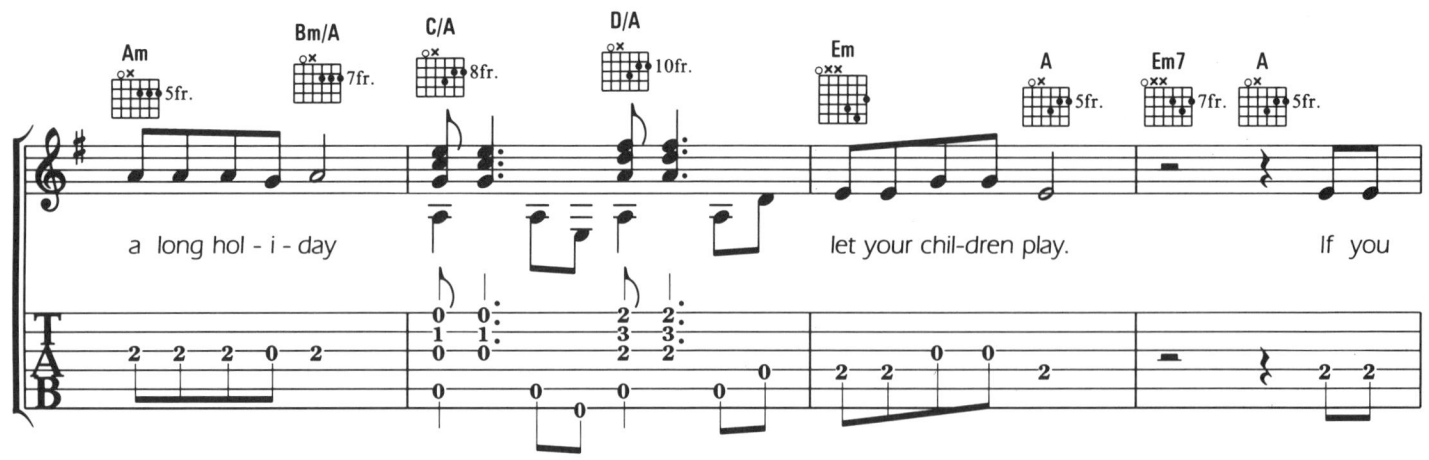
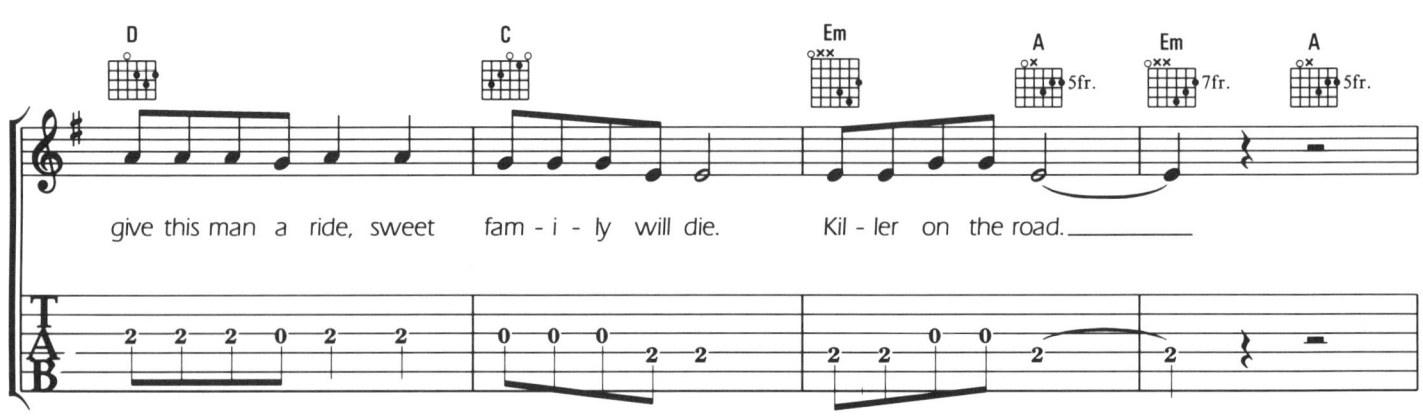
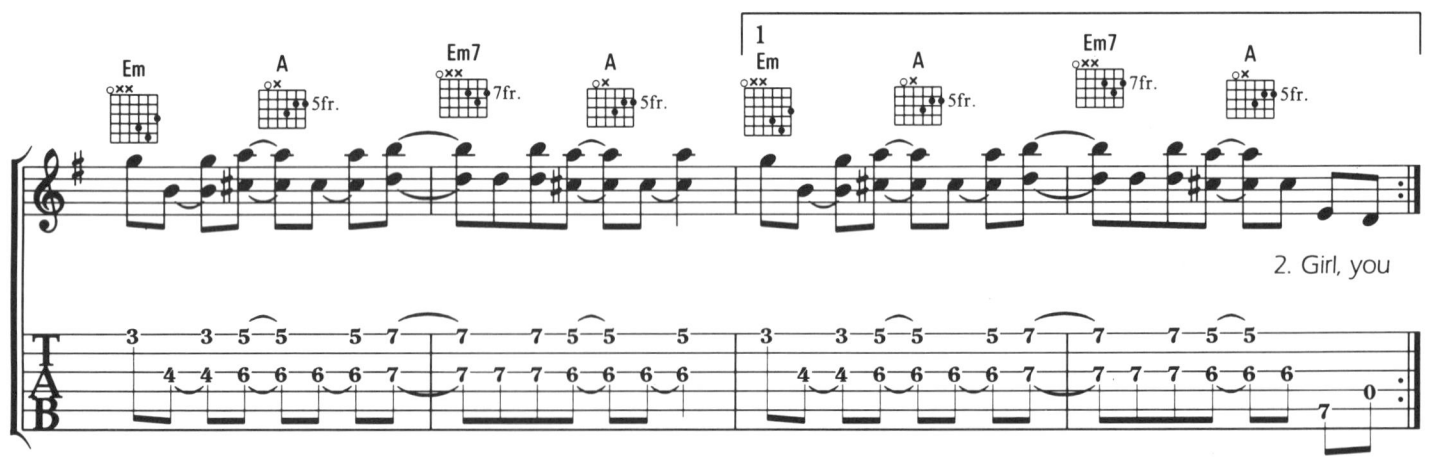
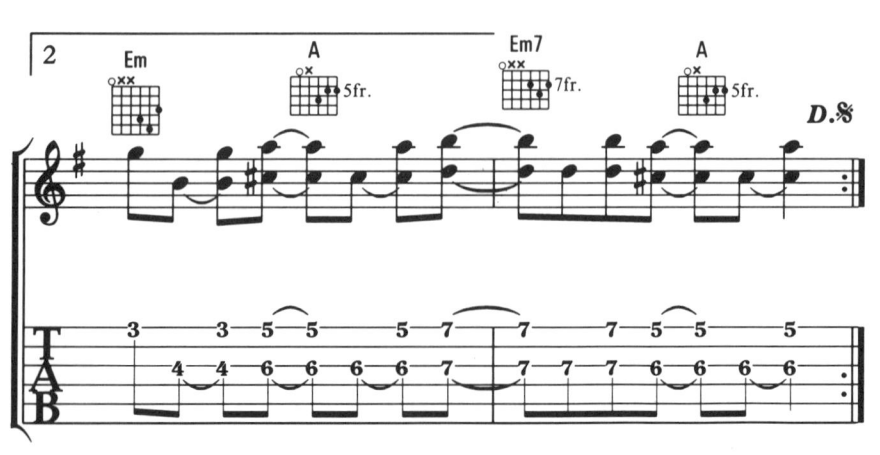
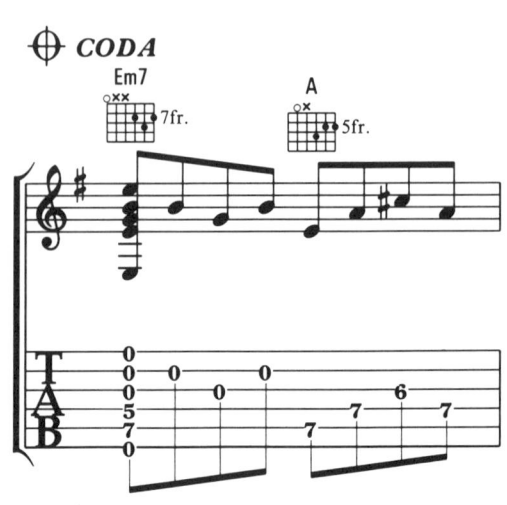

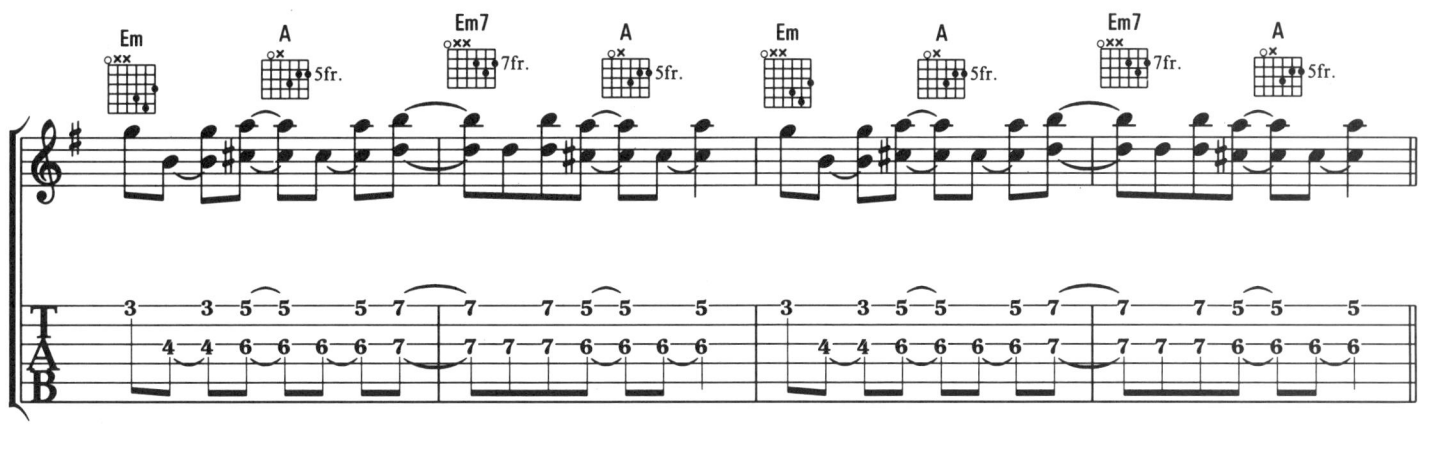
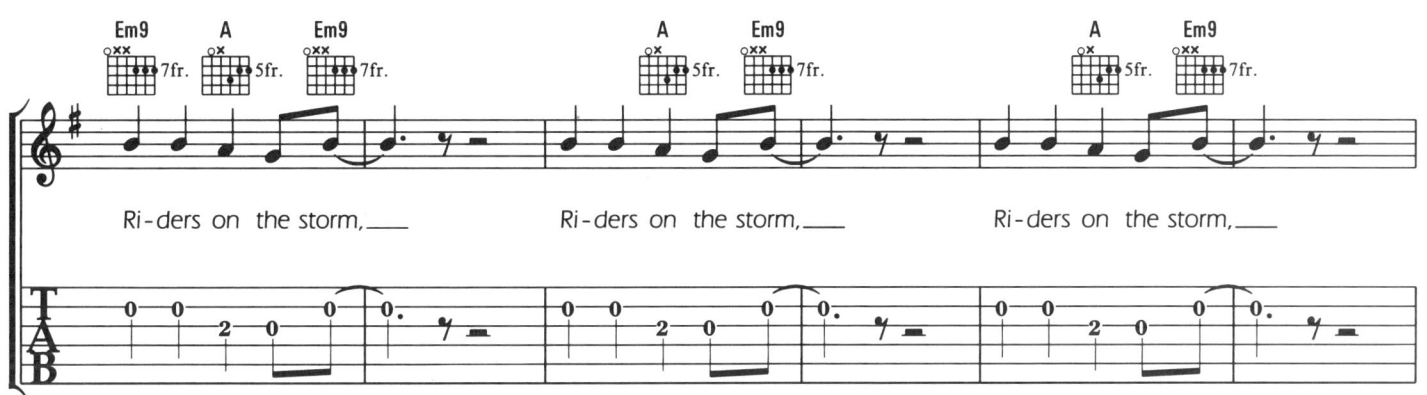
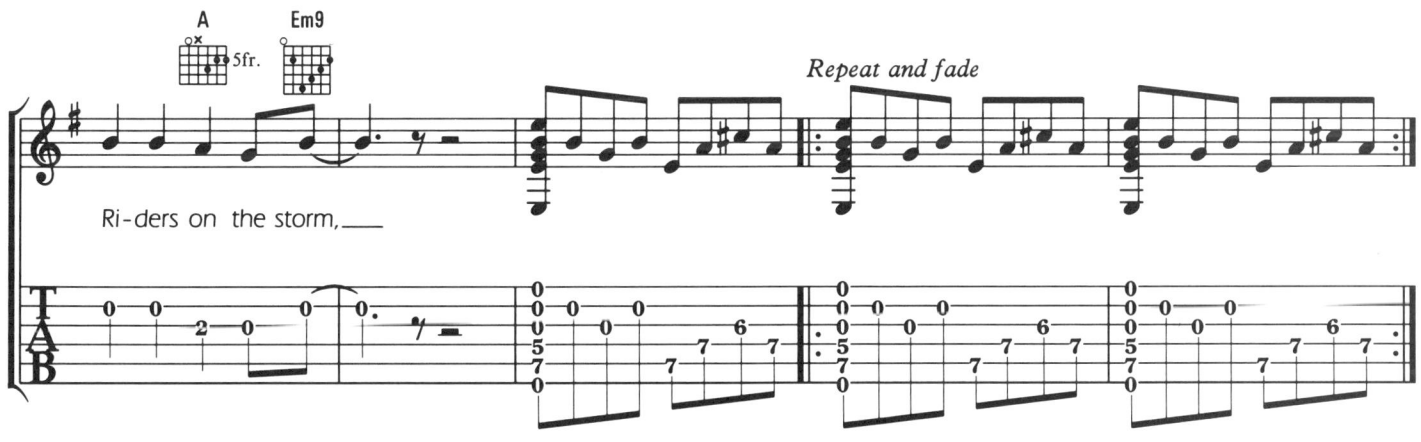

2 Girl you gotta love your man.
   girl, you gotta love your man.
   Take him by the hand,
   Make him understand.
   The world on you depends,
   our life will never end.
   You gotta love your man.

BEEN DOWN SO LONG

Words by Jim Morrison. Music by The Doors

© Copyright 1971 Doors Music Company, USA. All rights for the United Kingdom, Northern Ireland & Eire controlled by Rondor Music (London) Limited, 10a Parsons Green, London SW6.
All Rights Reserved. International Copyright Secured.

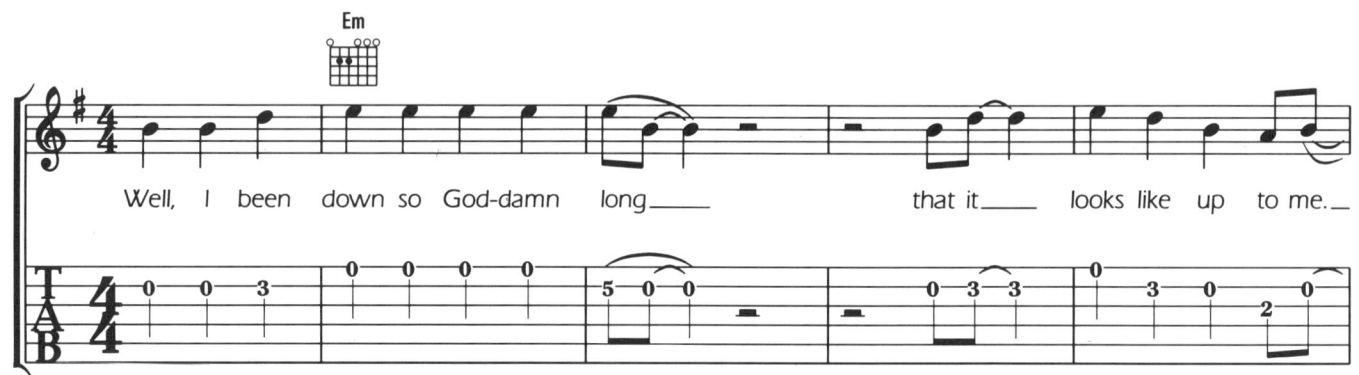

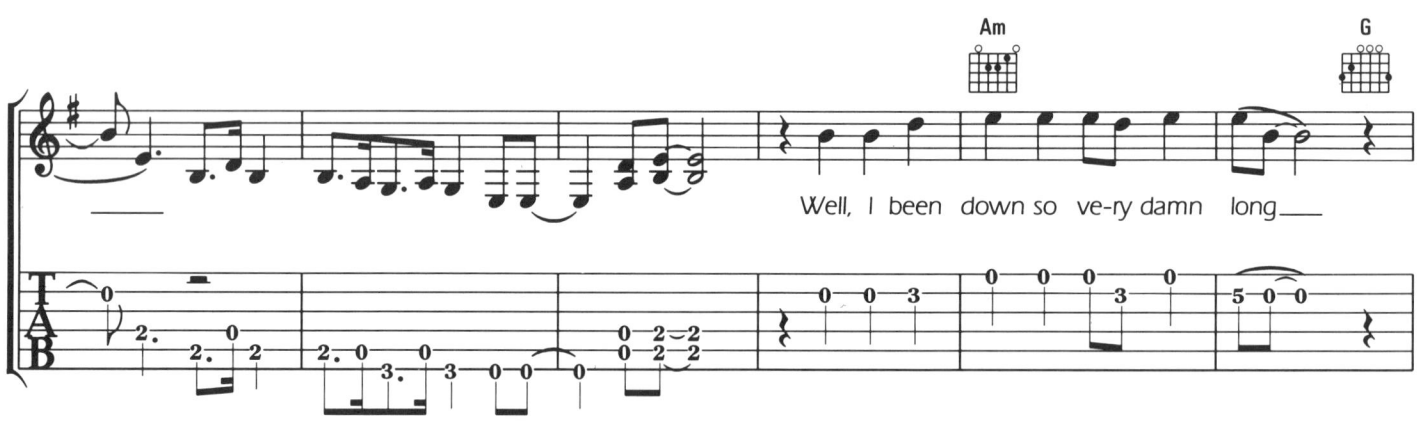

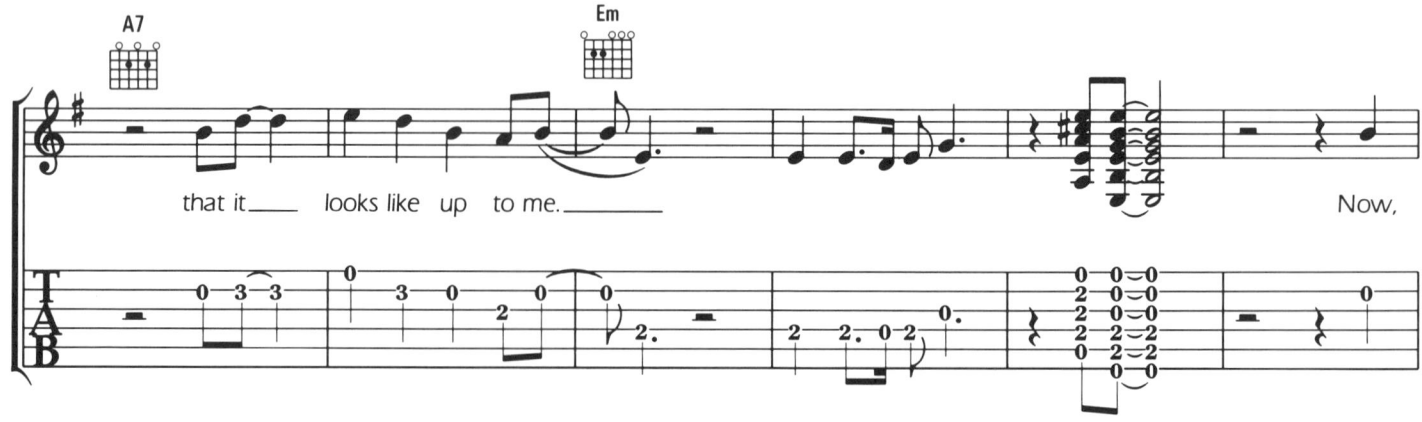

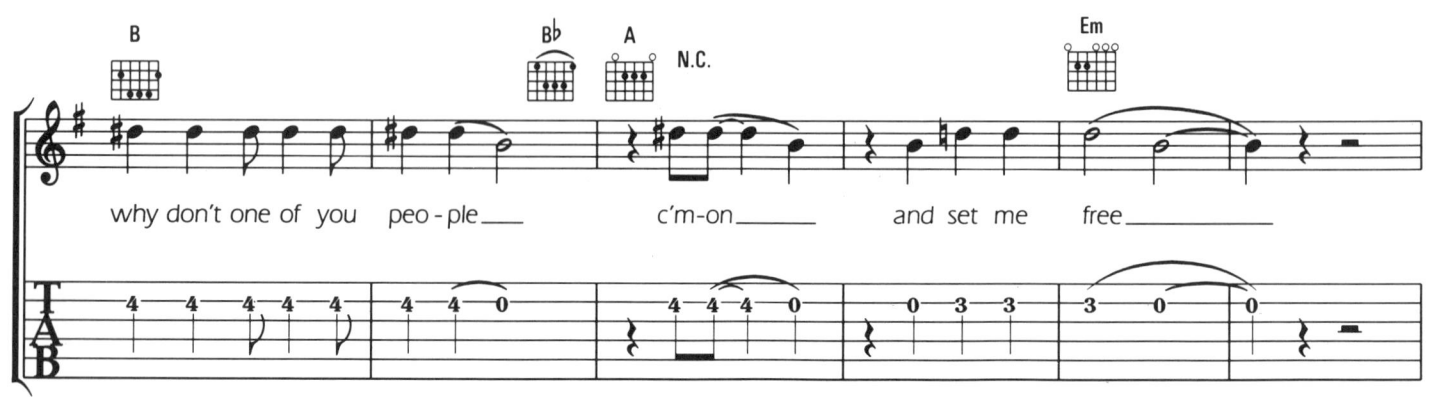

16

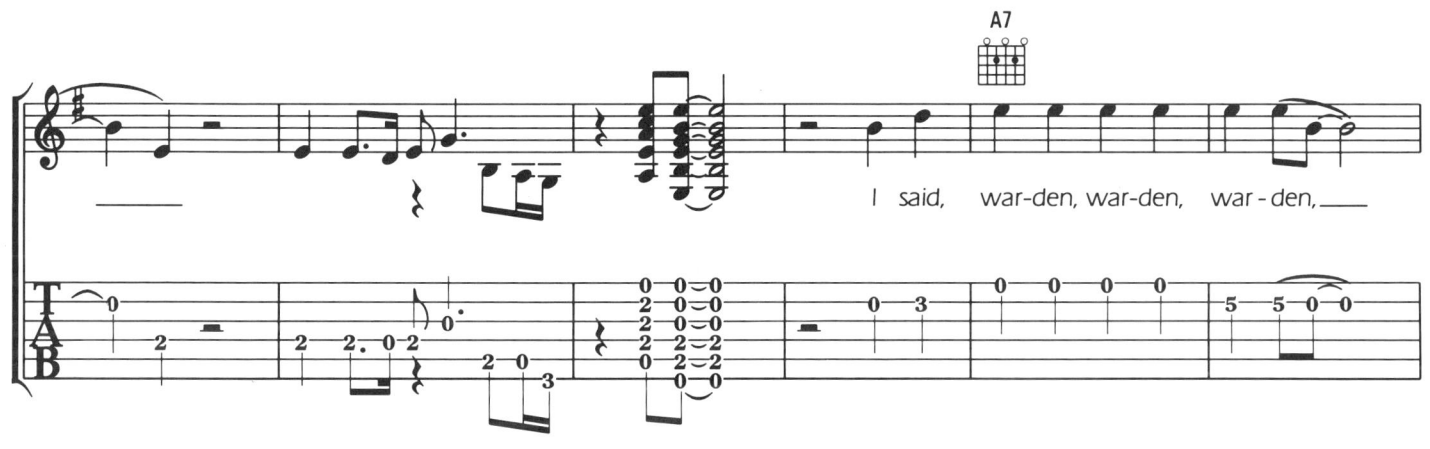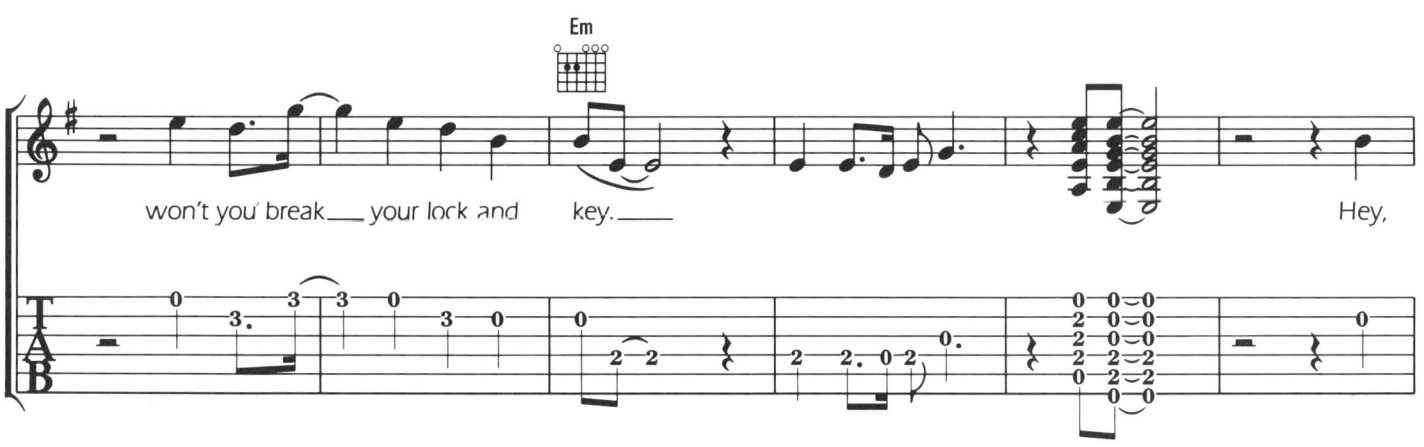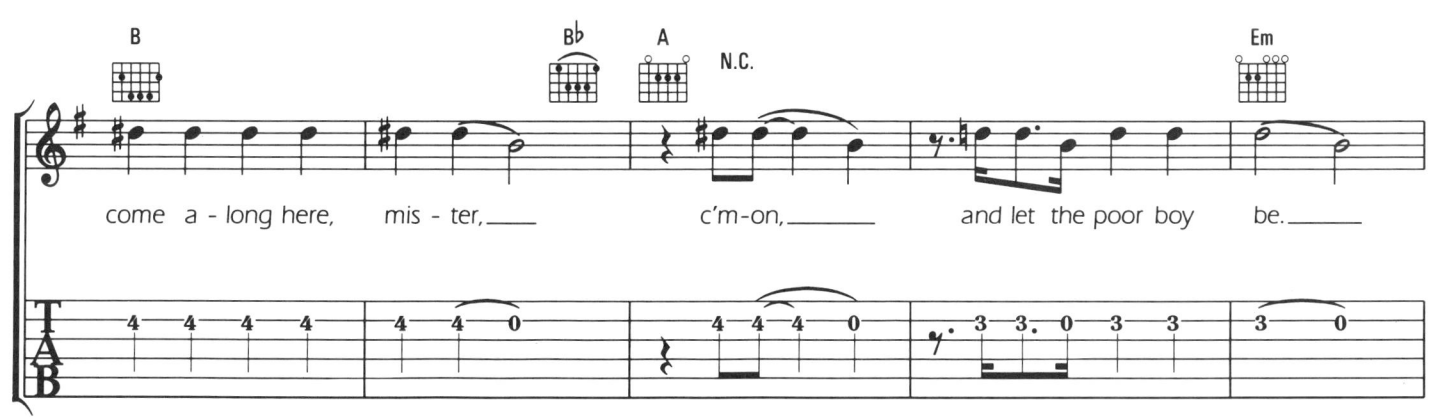

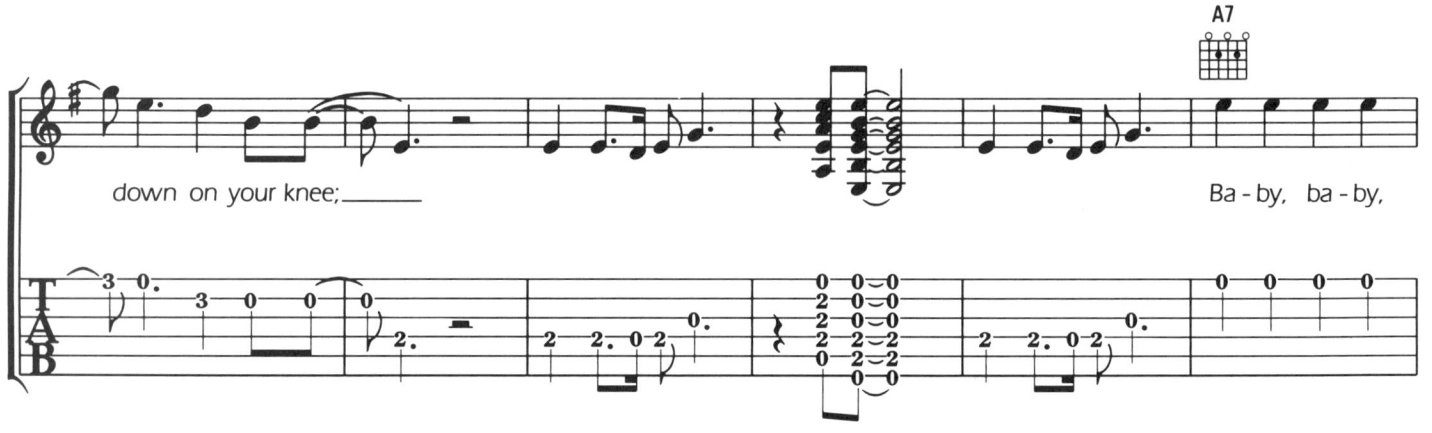
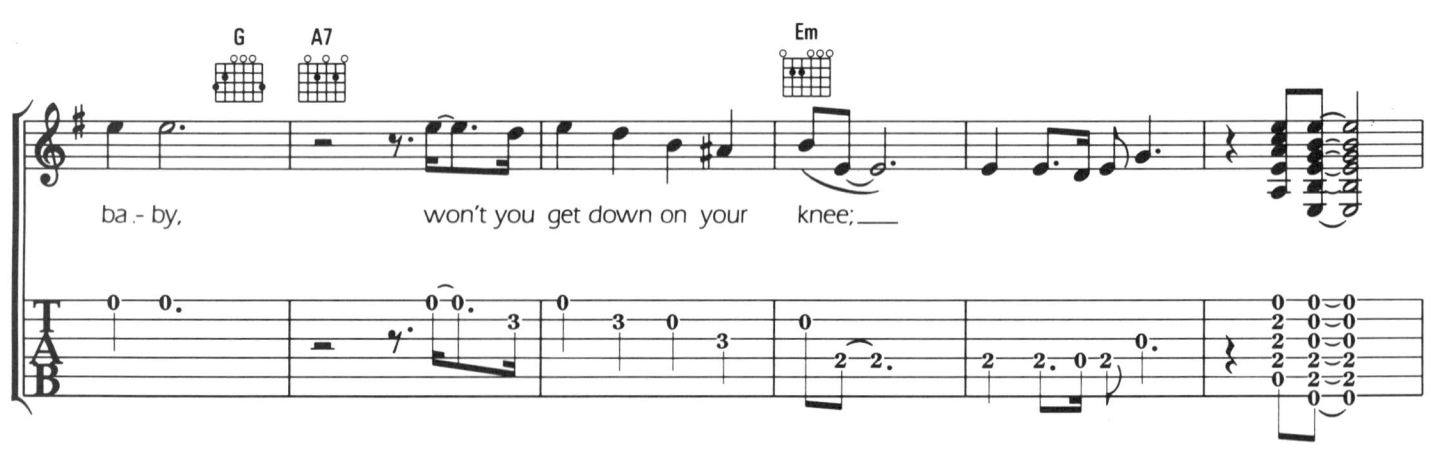
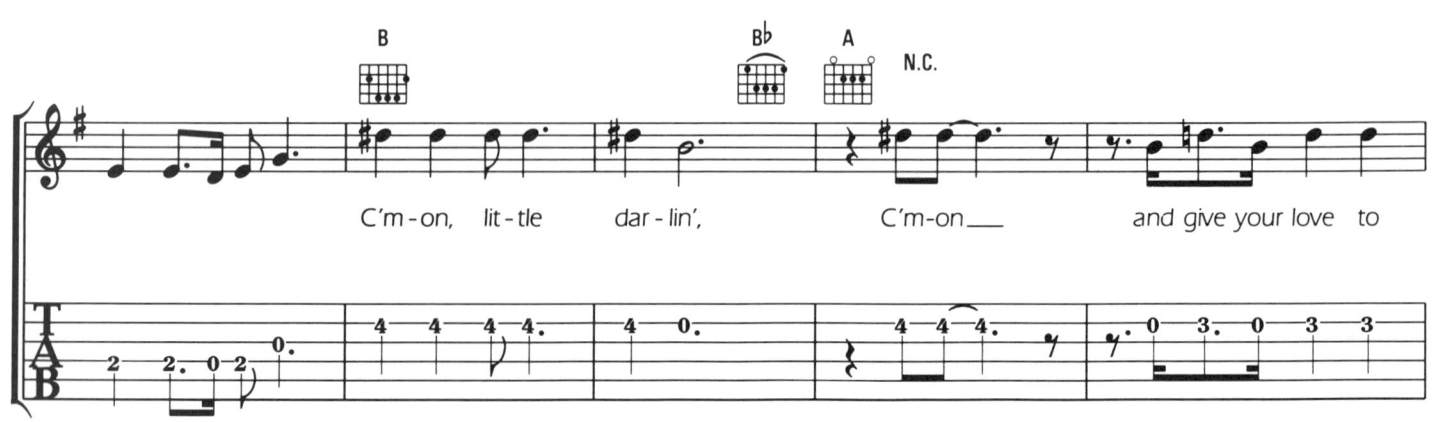

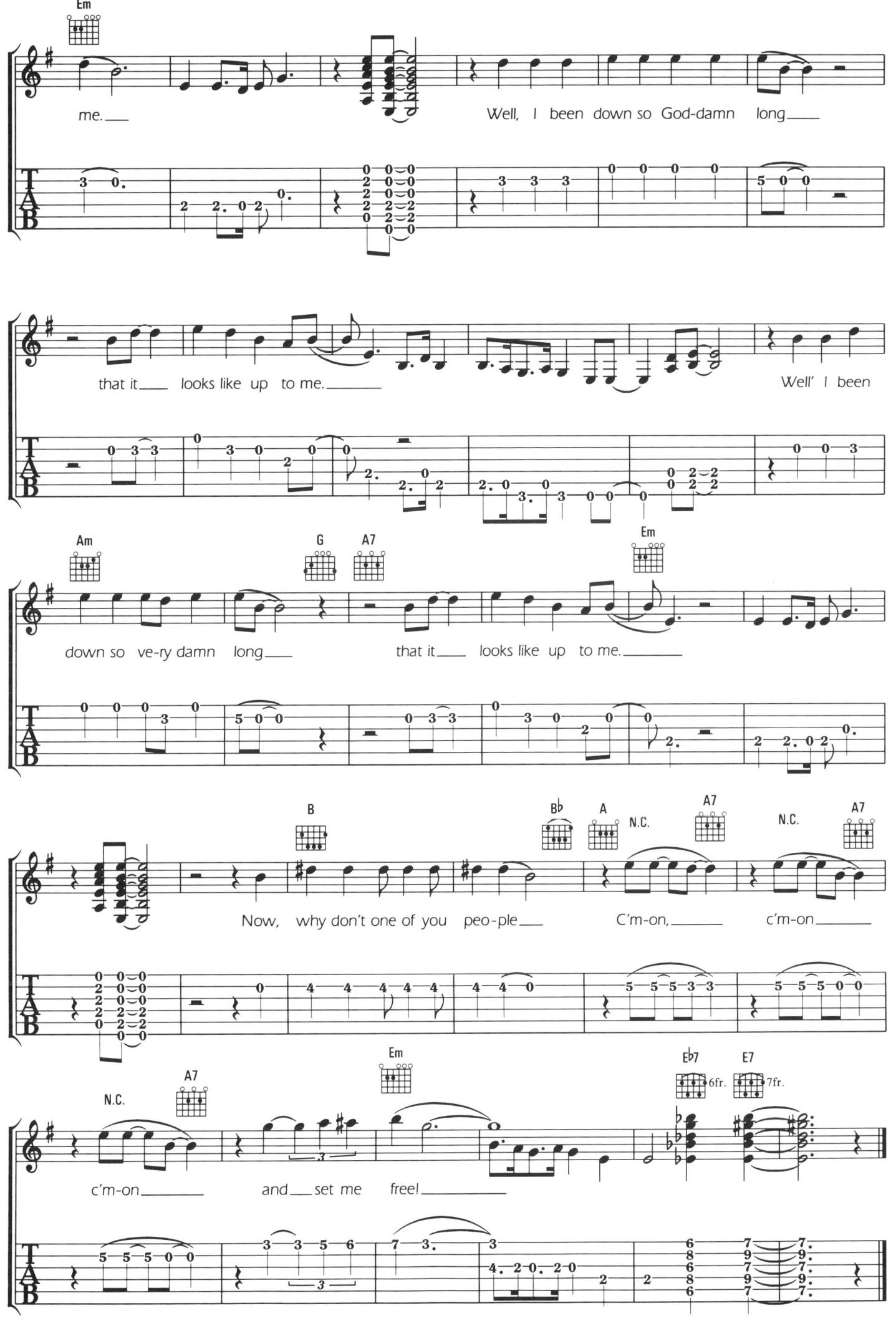

LOVE HER MADLY

Music by The Doors. Words by Robbie Krieger

© Copyright 1971 Doors Music Company, USA. All rights for the United Kingdom, Northern Ireland & Eire controlled by Rondor Music (London) Limited, 10a Parsons Green, London SW6.
All Rights Reserved. International Copyright Secured.

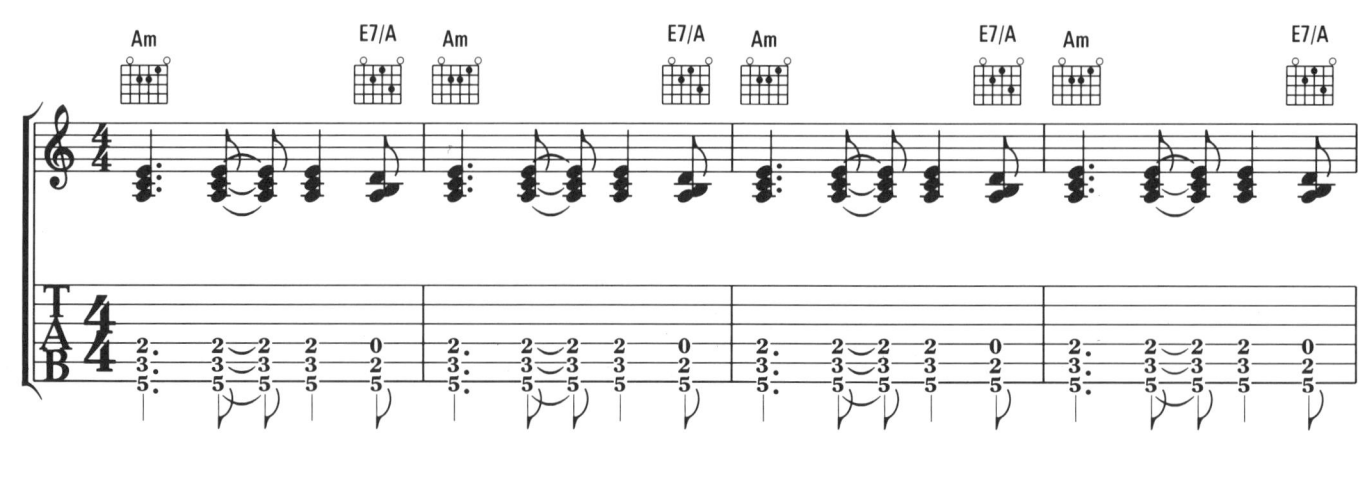
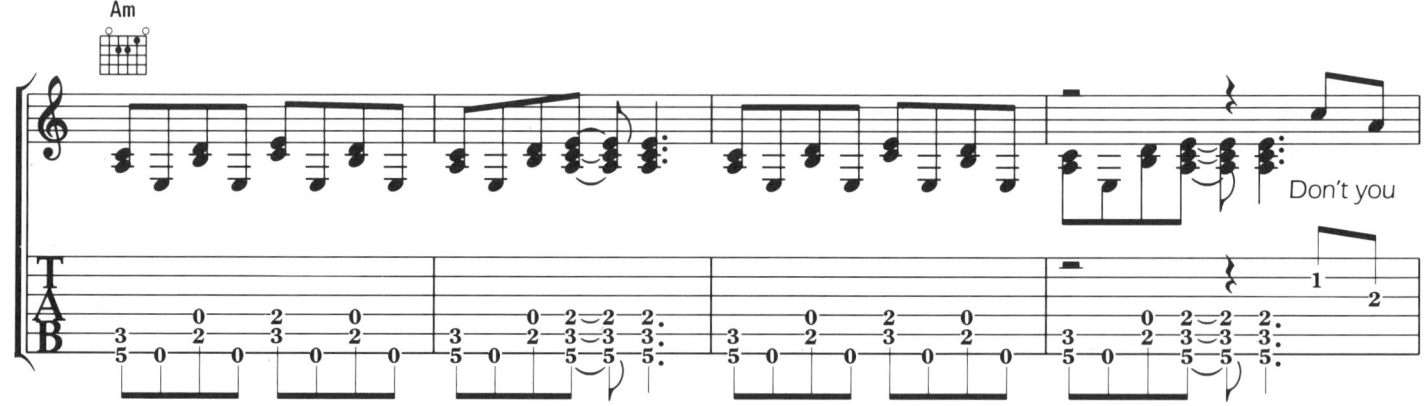

STRANGE DAYS

Words & Music by The Doors

© Copyright 1967 Doors Music Company, USA. All rights for the United
Kingdom, Northern Ireland & Eire controlled by Rondor Music (London)
Limited, 10a Parsons Green, London SW6.
All Rights Reserved. International Copyright Secured.

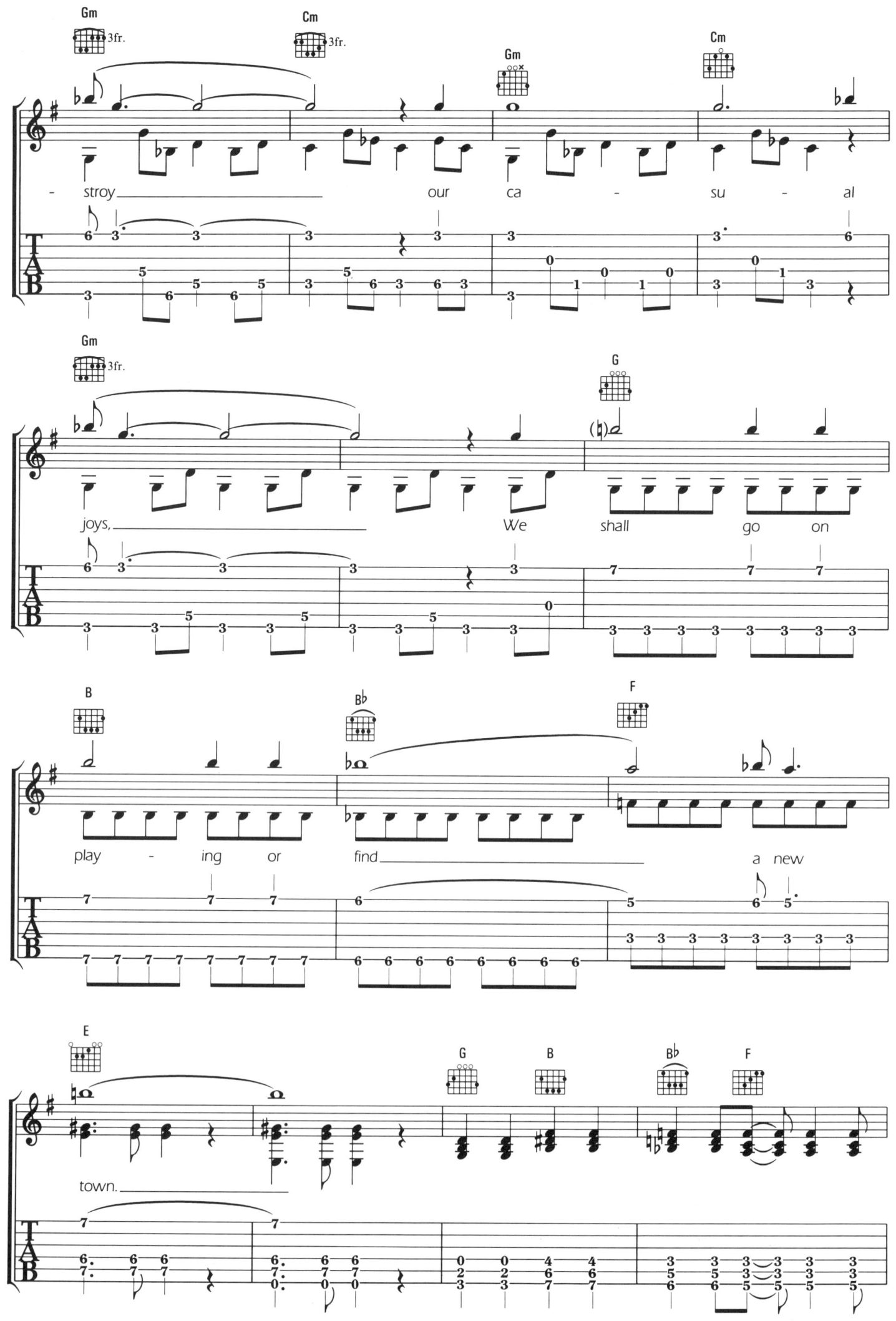

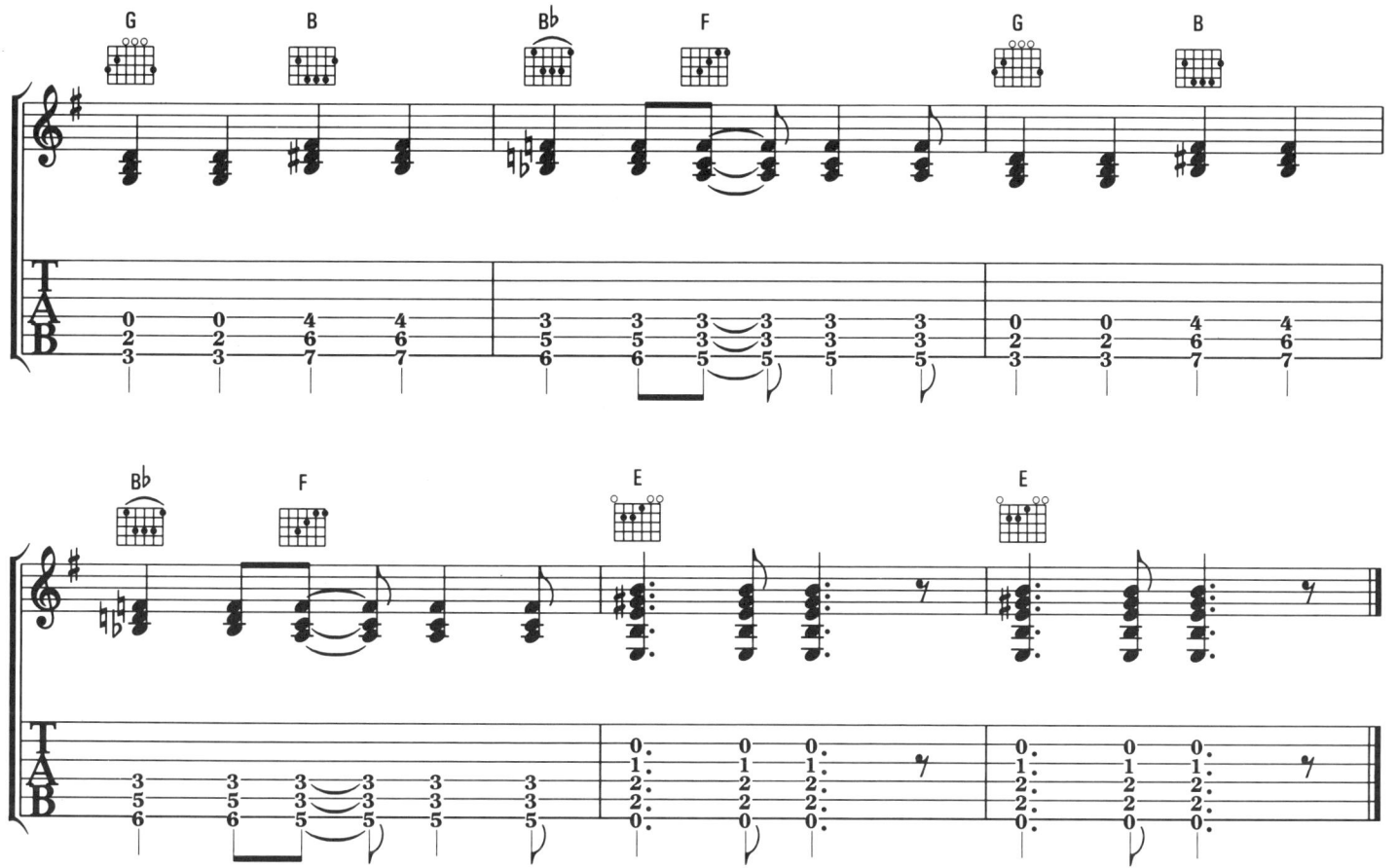

2 Strange eyes fill strange rooms,
   voices will signal their tired end,
   The hostess is grinning,
   her guests sleep from sinning,
   Hear me talk of sin and you know this is it.

3 Strange days have found us
   And through their strange hours
   We linger alone,
   Bodies confused,
   Memories misused,
   As we run from the day
   To a strange night of stone.

WHEN THE MUSIC'S OVER

Words & Music by The Doors

© Copyright 1967 Doors Music Company, USA. All rights for the United
Kingdom, Northern Ireland & Eire controlled by Rondor Music (London)
Limited, 10a Parsons Green, London SW6.
All Rights Reserved. International Copyright Secured.

Cancel my subscription to the resurrection,
send my credentials to the house of detention,
I got some friends inside.
The face in the mirror won't stop.
The girl in the window won't drop.
A feast of friends alive she cried,
waiting for me outside.

YOU'RE LOST, LITTLE GIRL

Words & Music by The Doors

© Copyright 1967 Doors Music Company, USA. All rights for the United
Kingdom, Northern Ireland & Eire controlled by Rondor Music (London)
Limited, 10a Parsons Green, London SW6.
All Rights Reserved. International Copyright Secured.

28

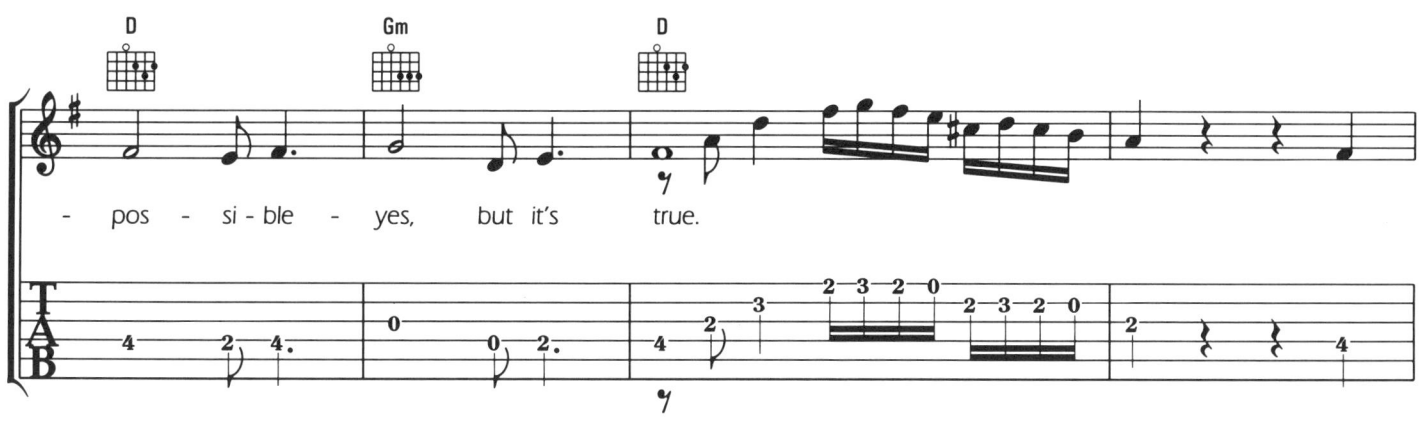
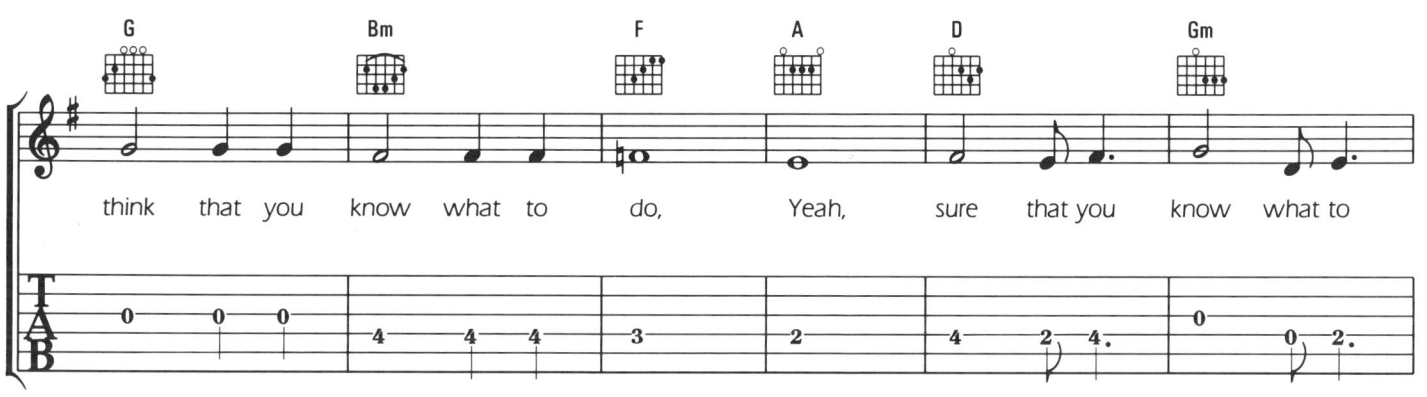
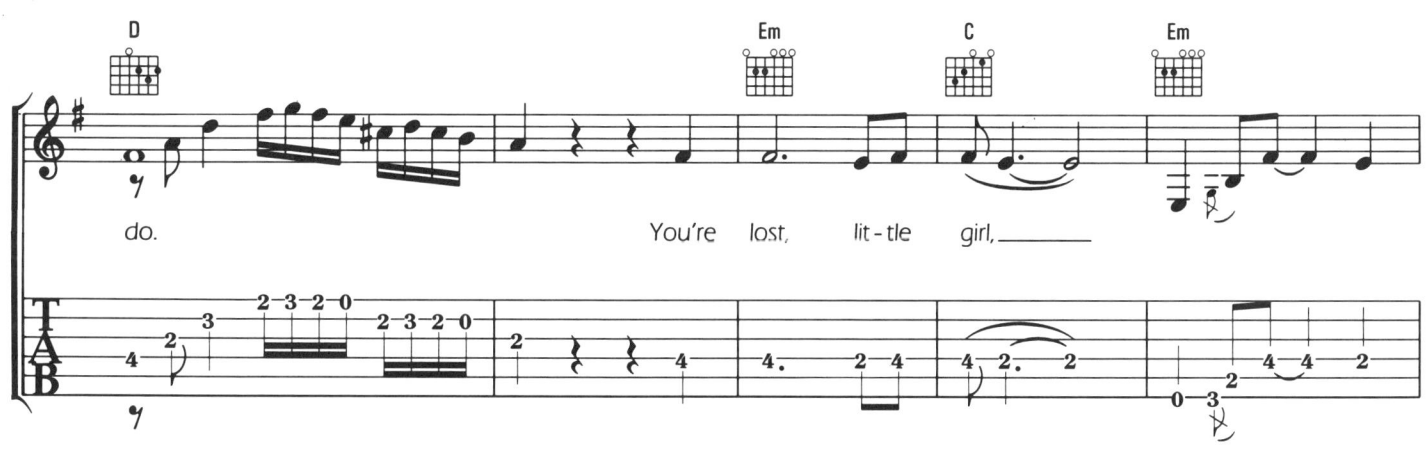
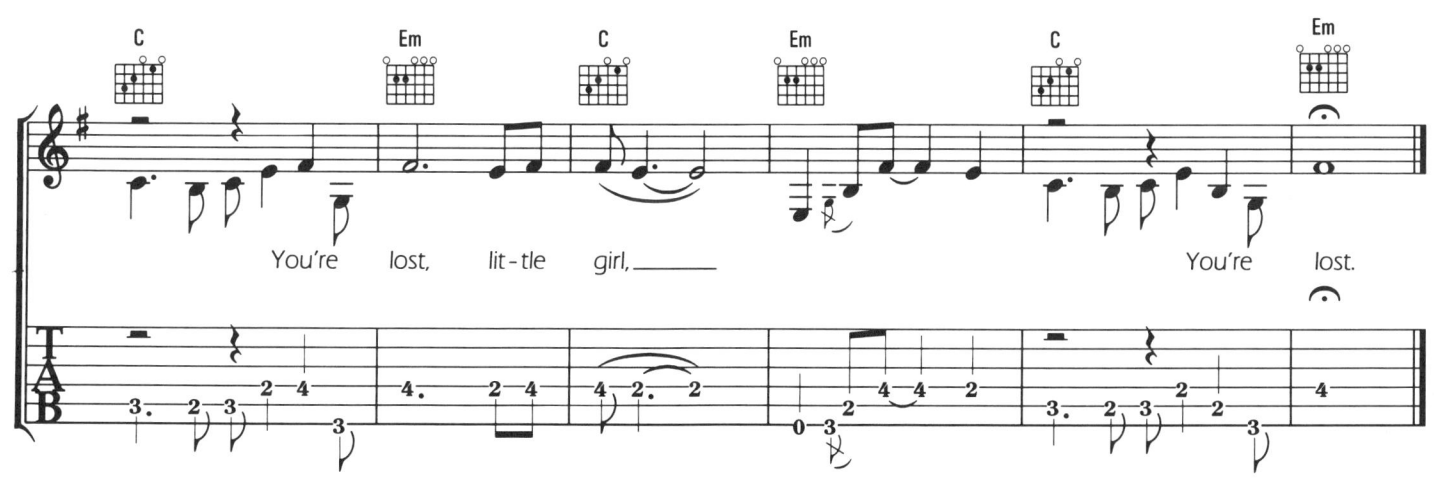

LOVE ME TWO TIMES

Words & Music by The Doors

© Copyright 1967 Doors Music Company, USA. All rights for the United Kingdom, Northern Ireland & Eire controlled by Rondor Music (London) Limited, 10a Parsons Green, London SW6.
All Rights Reserved. International Copyright Secured.

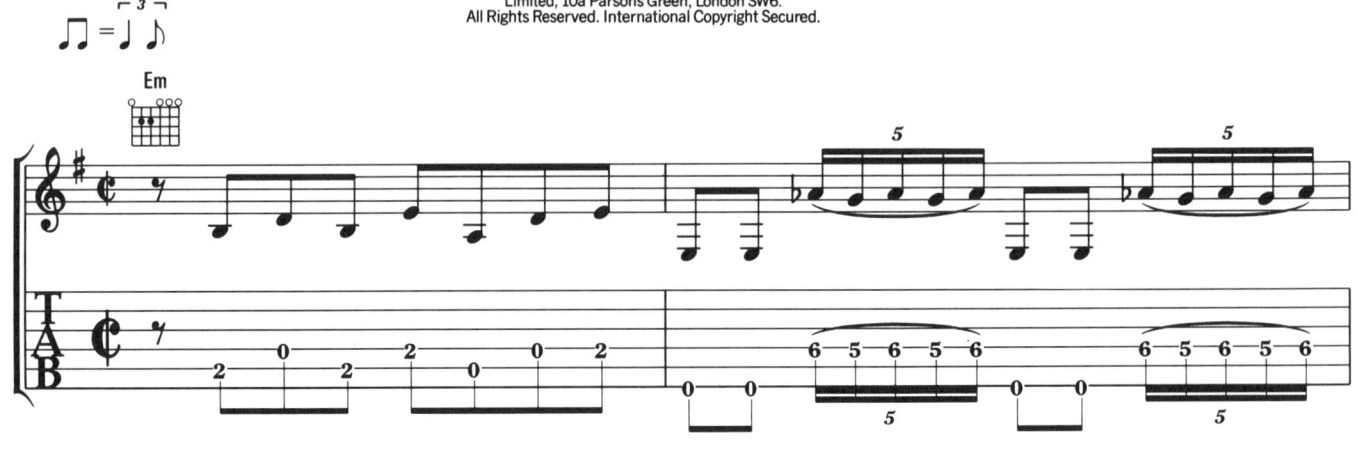
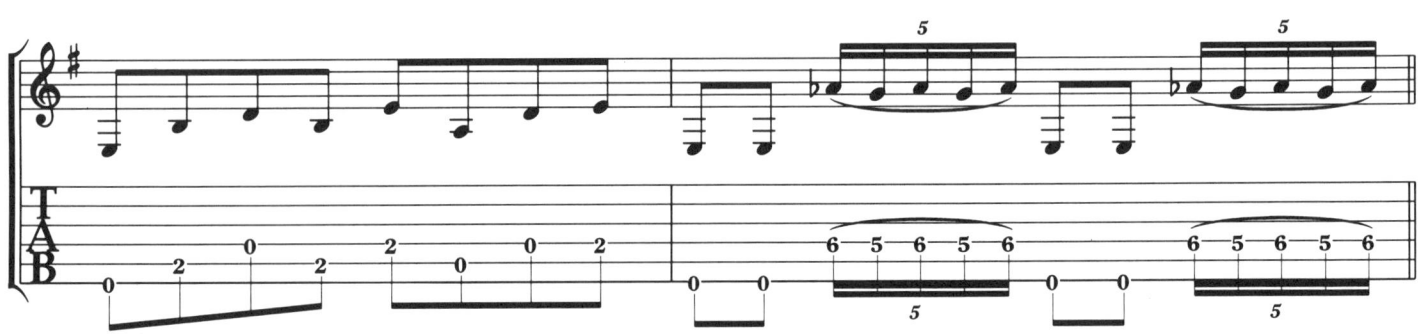
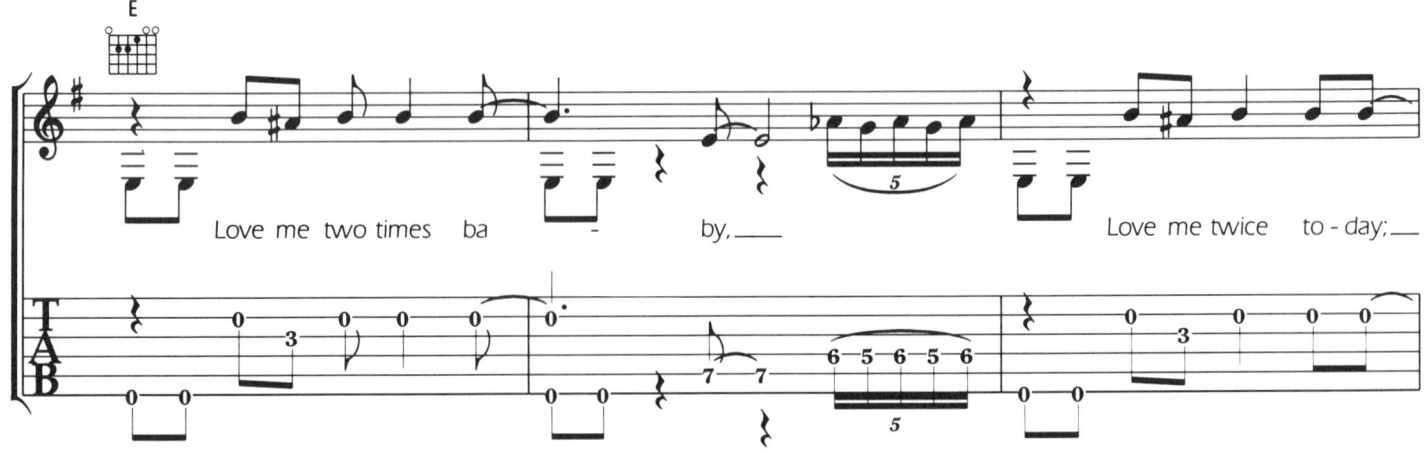

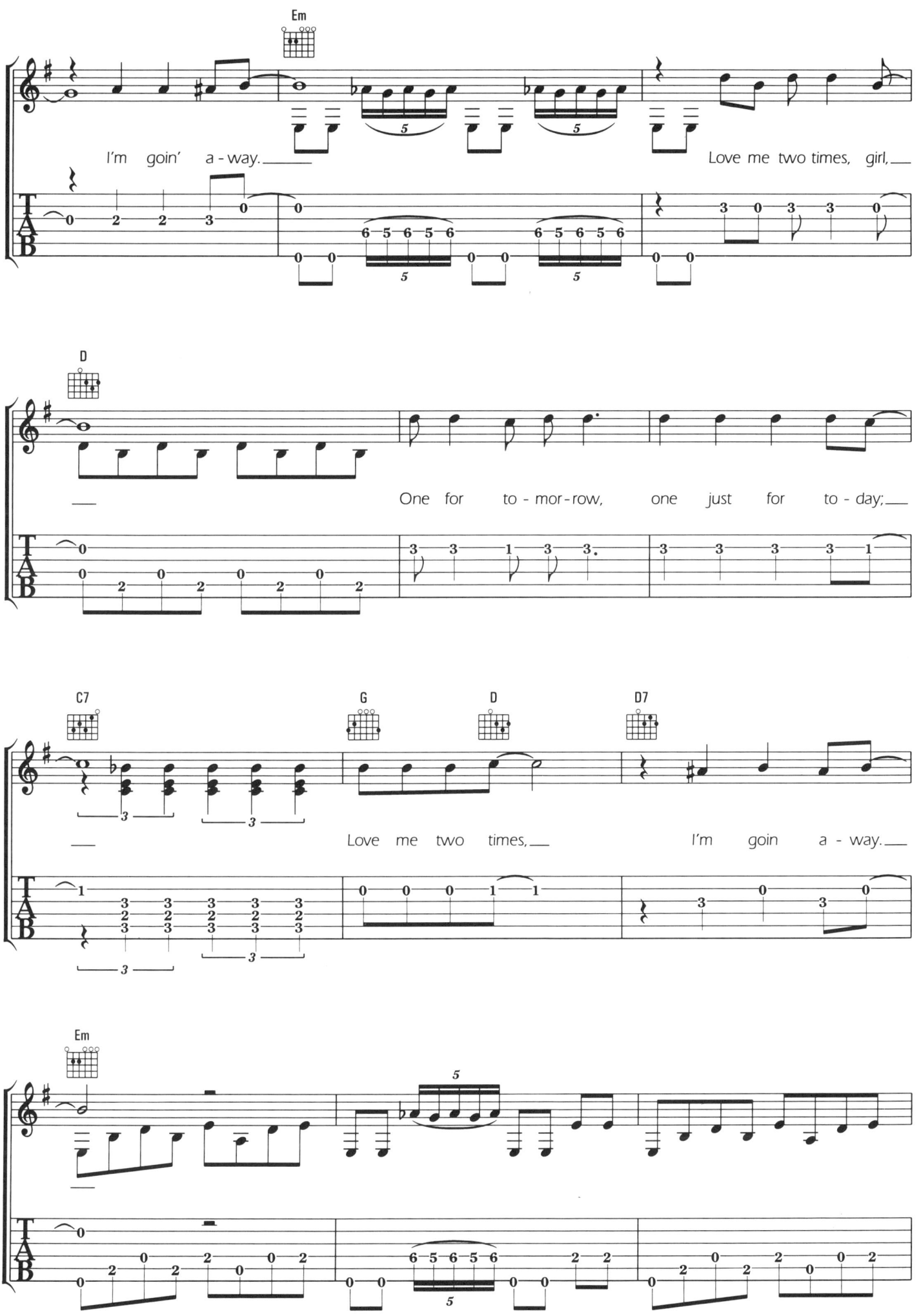

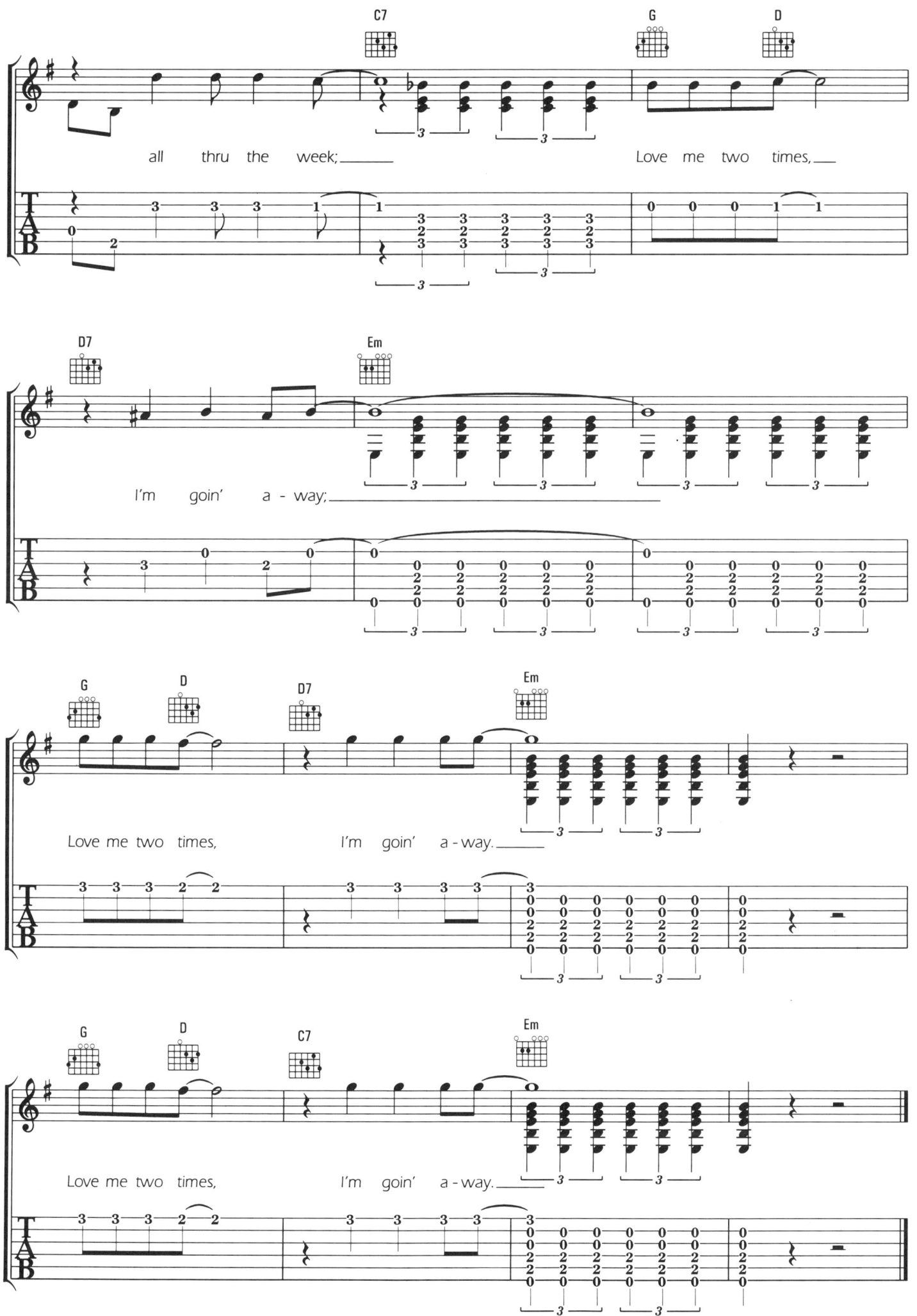

THE CRYSTAL SHIP

Words & Music by The Doors

© Copyright 1967 Doors Music Company, USA. All rights for the United Kingdom, Northern Ireland & Eire controlled by Rondor Music (London) Limited, 10a Parsons Green, London SW6.
All Rights Reserved. International Copyright Secured.

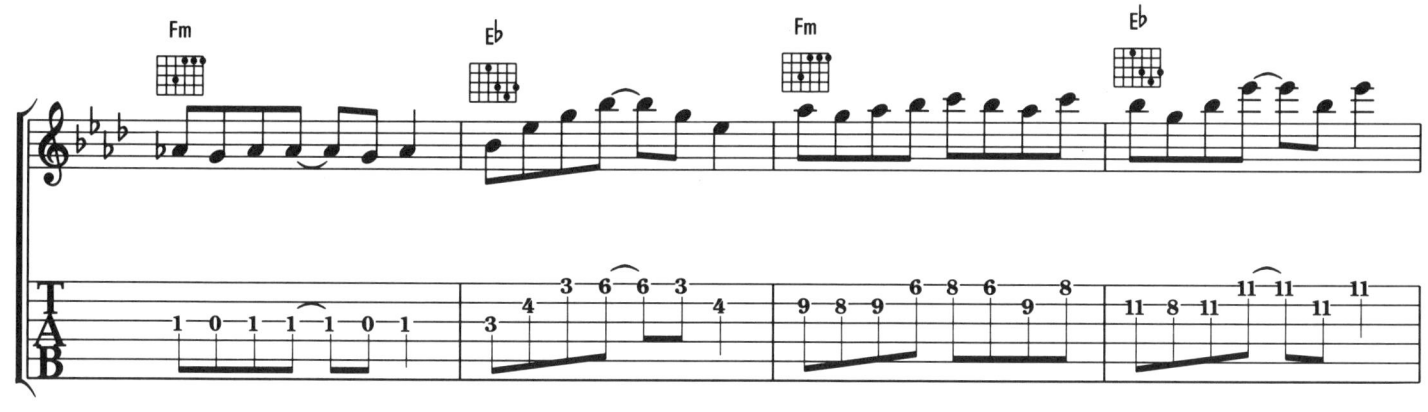
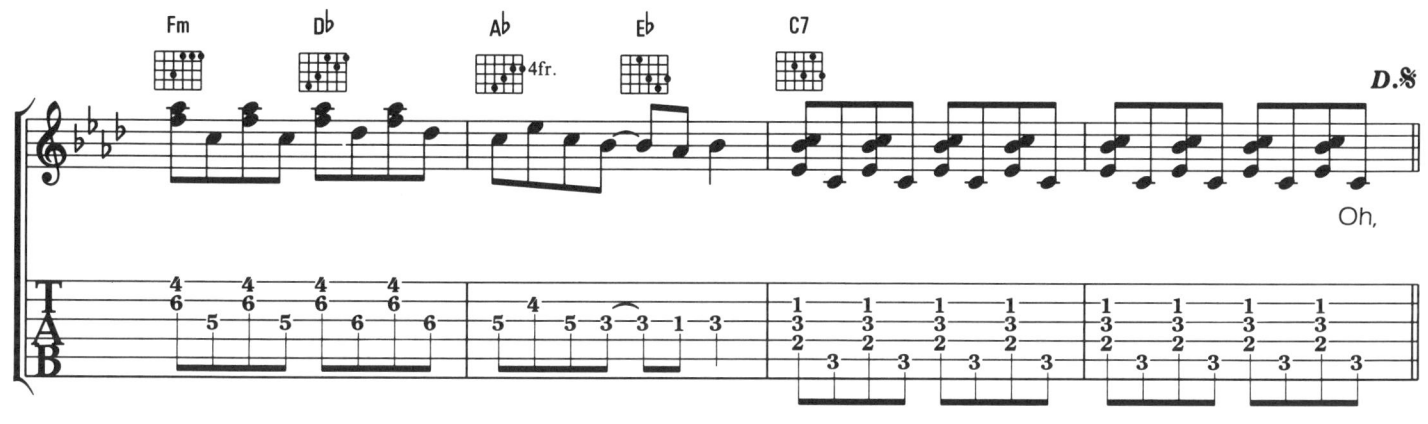
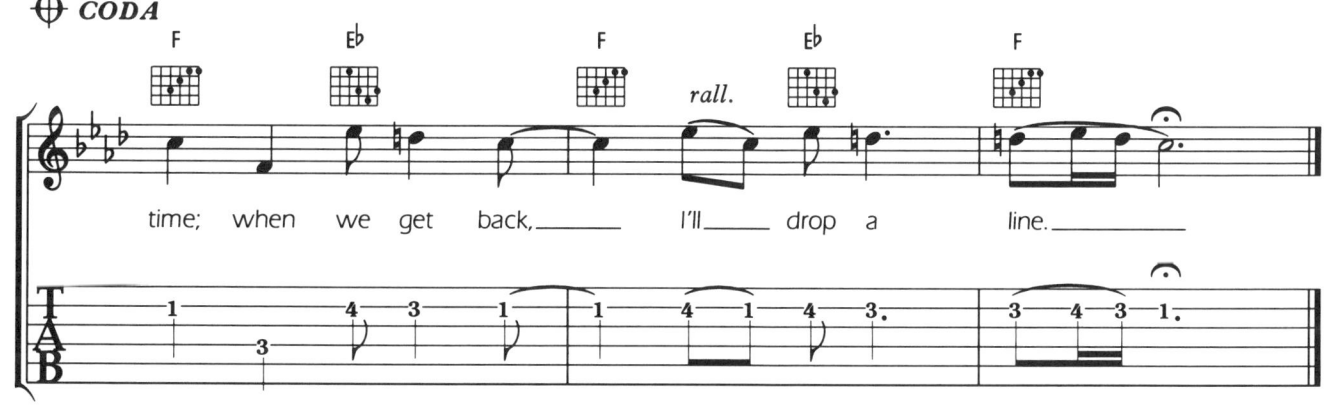

2. The days are bright and filled with pain.
   Enclose me in your gentle rain,
   The time you ran was too insane,
   we'll meet again, we'll meet again.

3. Oh, tell me where your freedom lies,
   The streets are fields that never die,
   Deliver me from reasons why
   You'd rather cry, I'd rather fly.

4. The crystal ship is being filled,
   A thousand girls, a thousand thrills,
   A million ways to spend your time;
   When we get back, I'll drop a line.

L.A. Woman

Words & Music by The Doors

© Copyright 1971 Doors Music Company, USA. All rights for the United Kingdom, Northern Ireland & Eire controlled by Rondor Music (London) Limited, 10a Parsons Green, London SW6.
All Rights Reserved. International Copyright Secured.

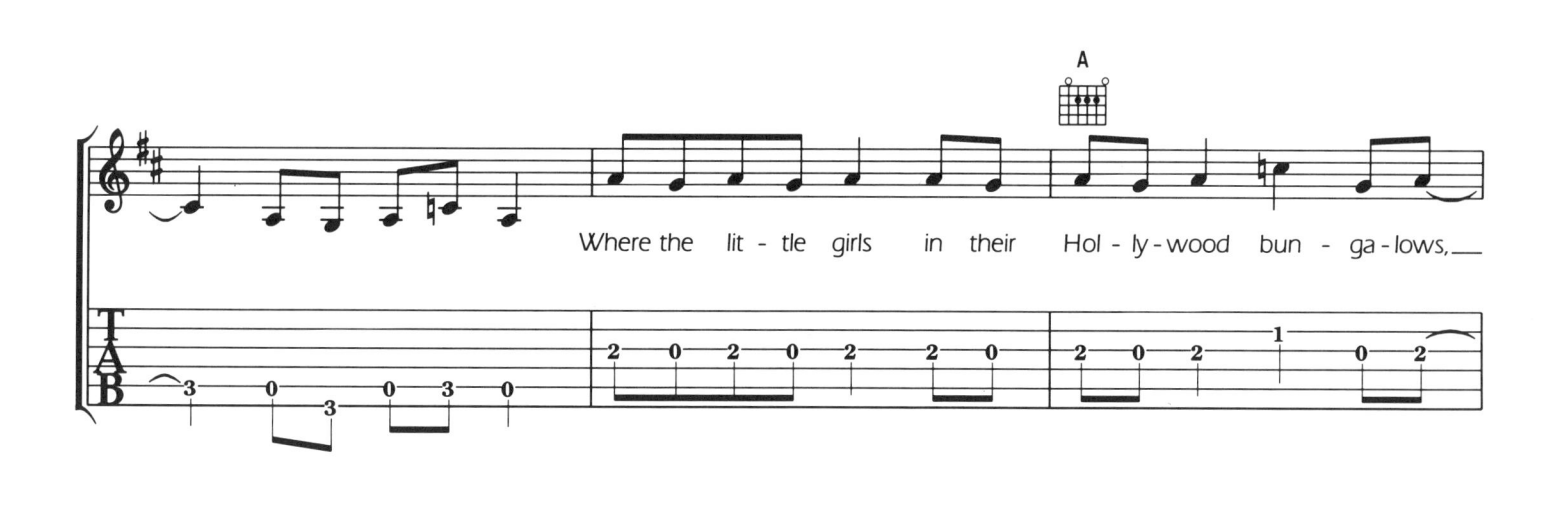

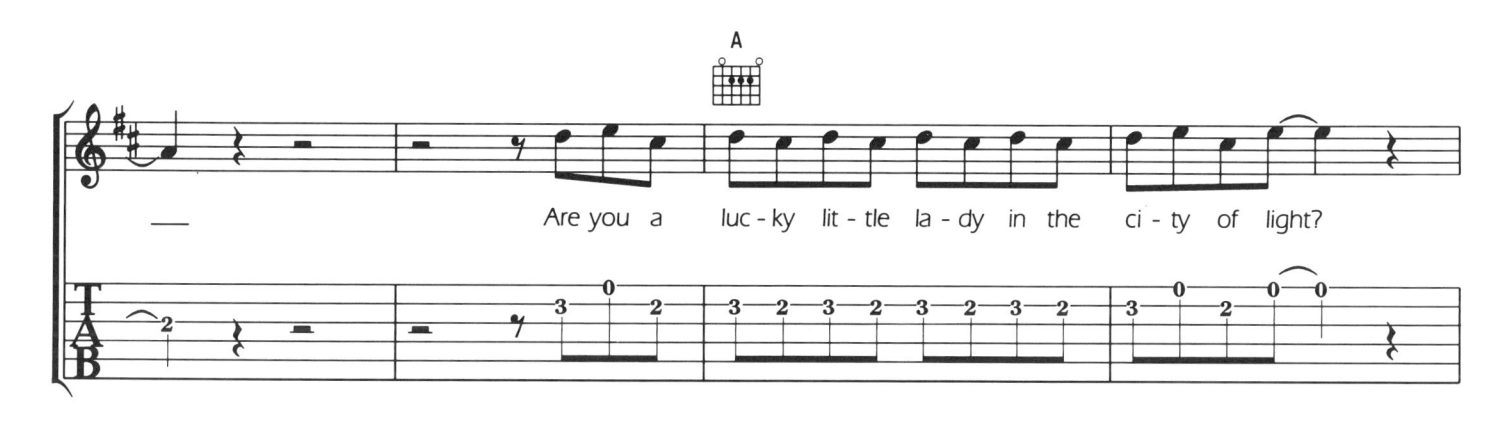

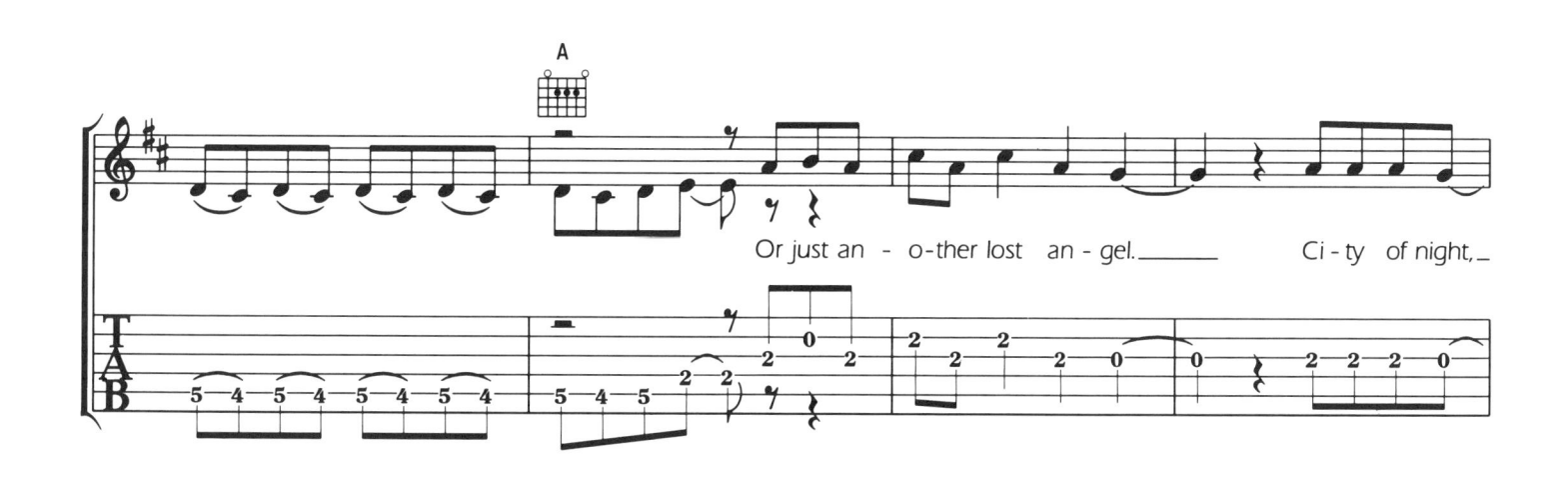

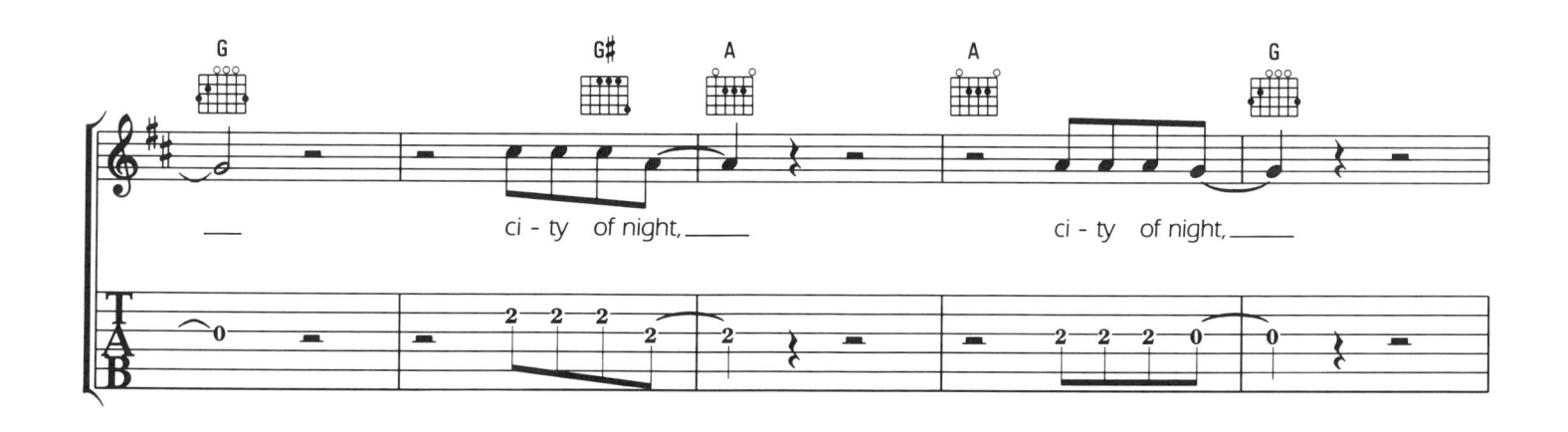

Where the lit-tle girls in their Hol-ly-wood bun-ga-lows,

Are you a luc-ky lit-tle la-dy in the ci-ty of light?

Or just an-o-ther lost an-gel. City of night,

ci-ty of night, ci-ty of night,

37

G♯
A
ci-ty of night.
L. A. wo-man,
L. A. wo-man,
A
L. A. wo - man, Sun-day
af - ter - noon,
L. A. wo - man, Sun-day
A
af - ter - noon,
A
L. A. wo - man, Sun-day

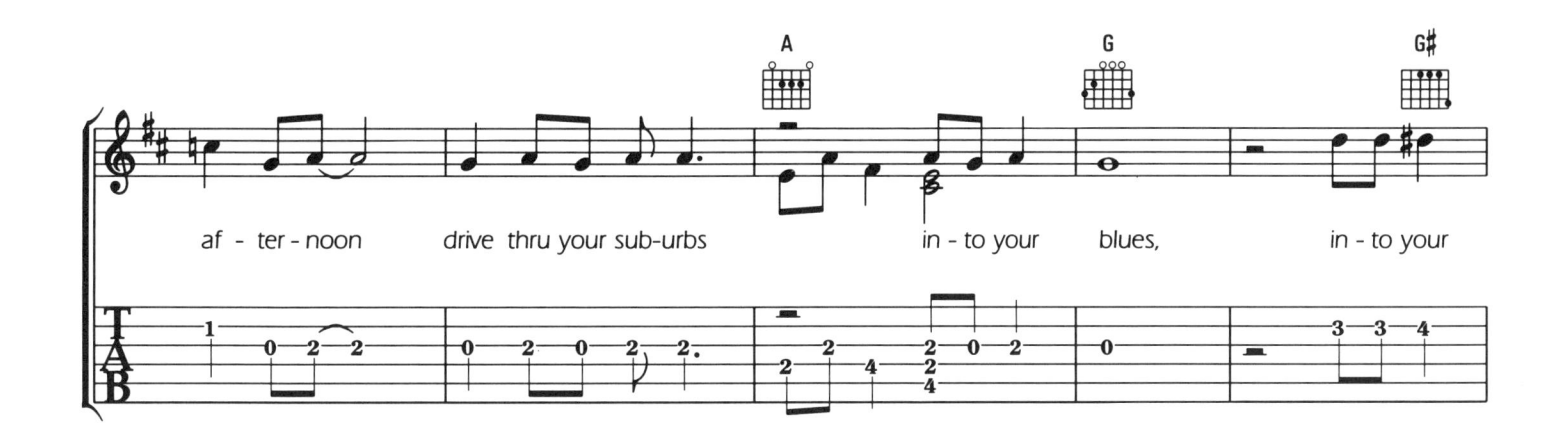

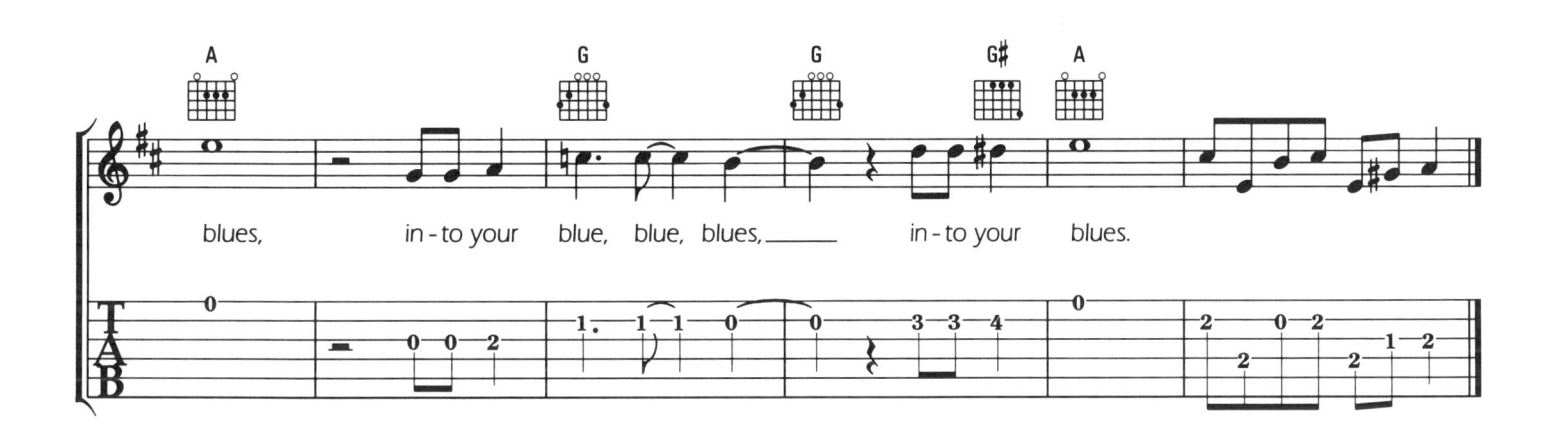

af - ter - noon drive thru your sub-urbs in - to your blues, in - to your blues, in - to your blue, blue, blues, in - to your blues.

I see your hair is burning,
Hills are filled with fire;
If they say I never loved you,
You know they are a liar.
Drivin' down the freeway,
Midnight alleys roam,
Cops in cars, topless bars,
Never saw a woman so alone,
So alone, so alone, so alone.
Motel money, murder madness,
Let's change the mood from glad to sadness.

Mister Mojo risin', Mister Mojo risin',
Got to keep on risin', Mister Mojo risin',
Mister Mojo risin', Mojo risin',
Mister Mojo risin', Mister Mojo risin',
Got ot keep on risin', risin', risin',
Risin', risin', risin', risin',
Risin', risin', risin', risin',
L. A. woman, L. A. woman.
She's my L. A. woman, L. A. woman.

LAND HO!

Music by The Doors. Words by Jim Morrison

© Copyright 1970 Doors Music Company, USA. All rights for the United
Kingdom, Northern Ireland & Eire controlled by Rondor Music (London)
Limited, 10a Parsons Green, London SW6.
All Rights Reserved. International Copyright Secured.

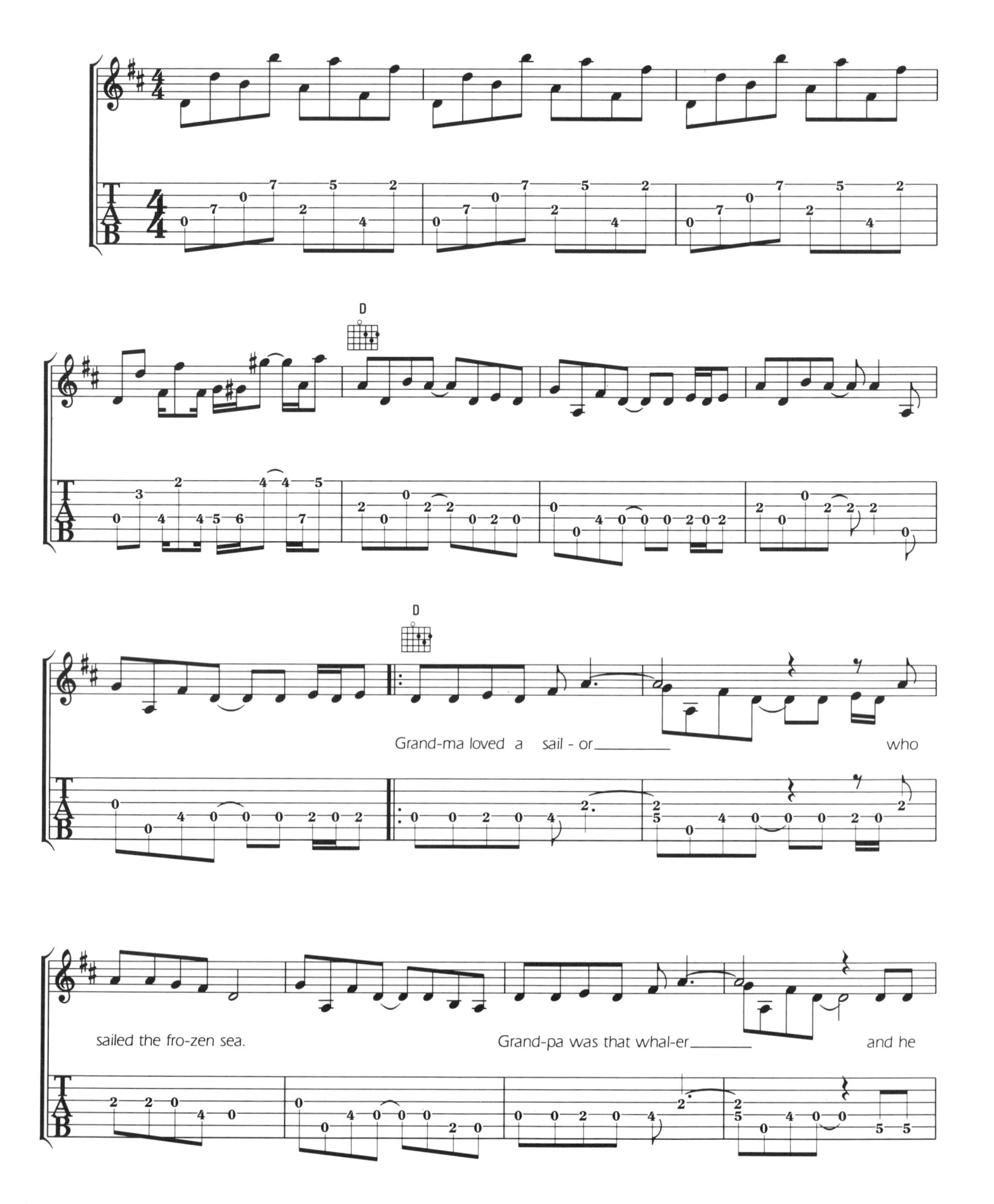

Grand-ma loved a sail-or_____ who sailed the fro-zen sea. Grand-pa was that whal-er_____ and he

took me on his knee. He said, 'Son, I'm go-in' cra-zy from liv-in' on the land. Got to find my ship-mates and walk on foreign sands.'

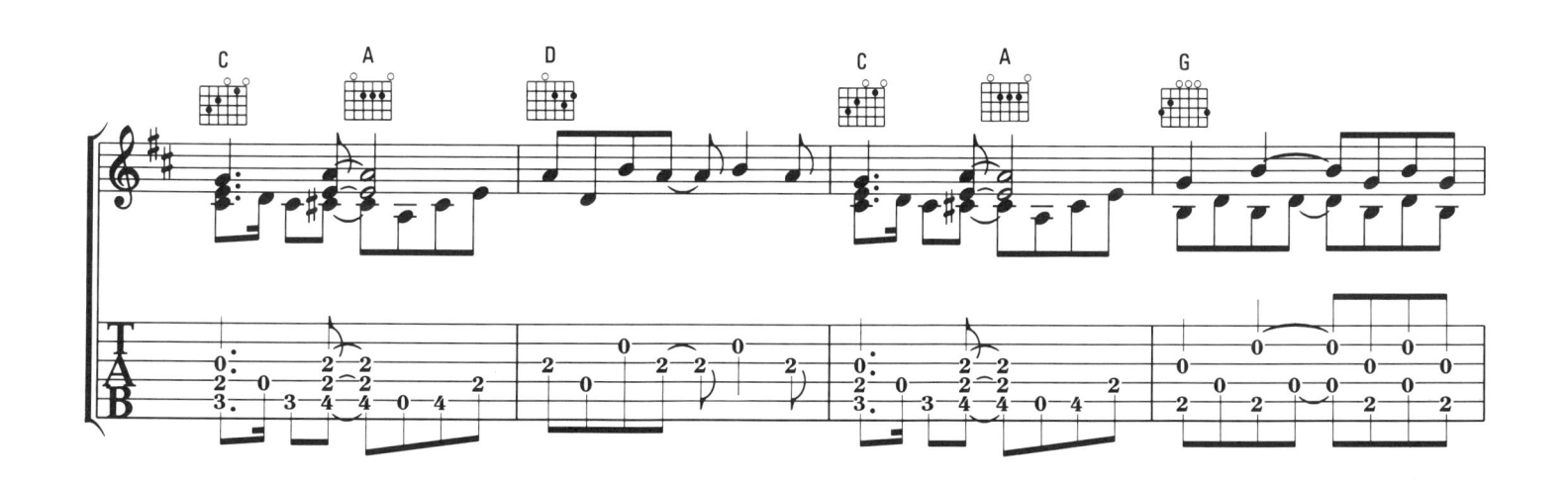

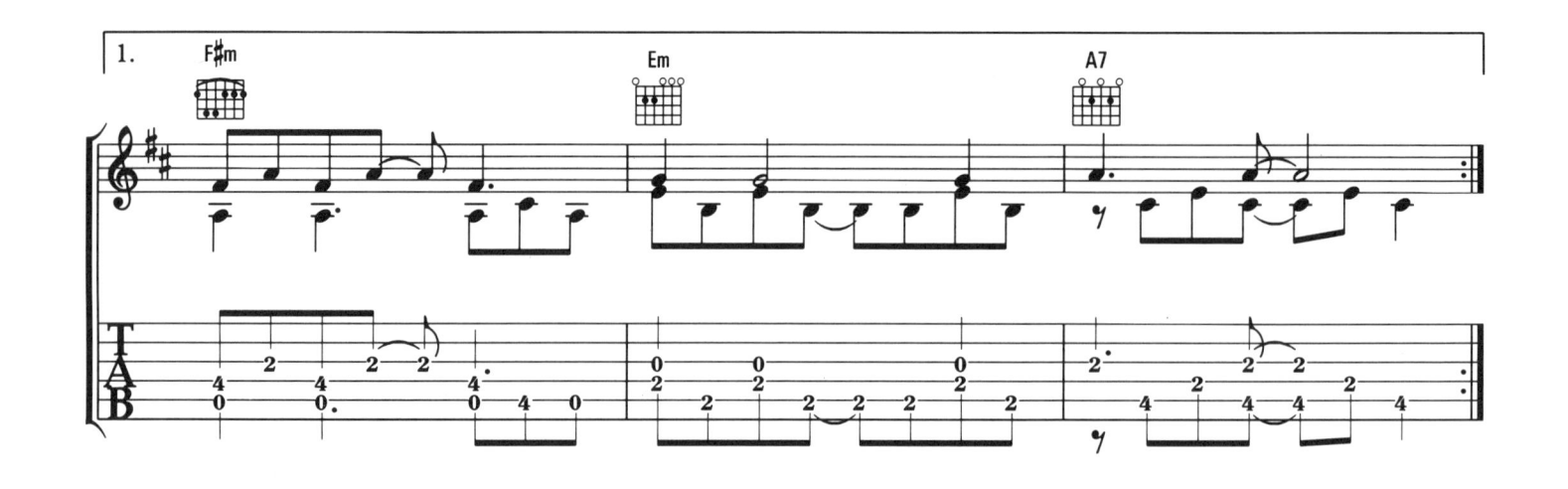

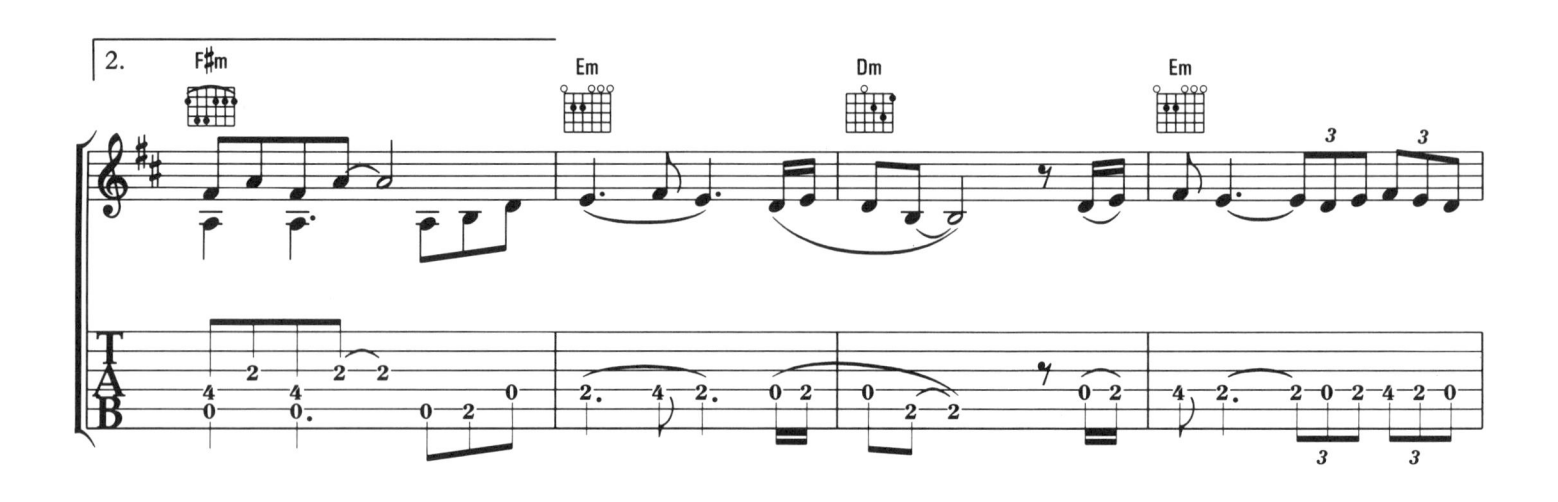

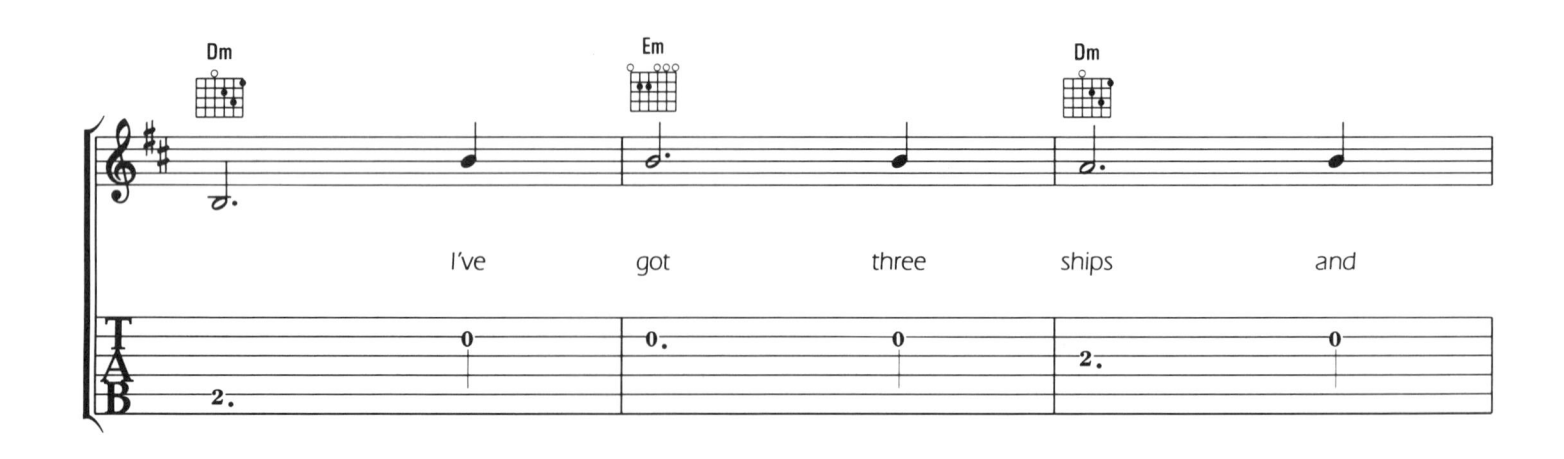

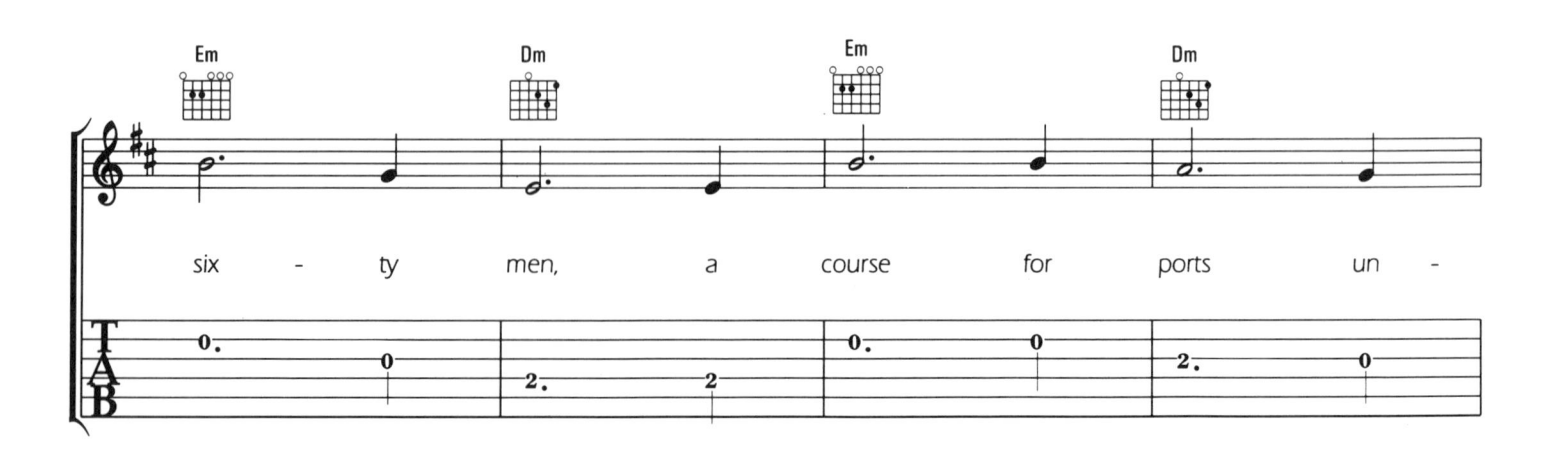

Lyrics: I've got three ships and sixty men, a course for ports un-

-read. Land Ho!

(S. Drum: Cross 5th and 6th string at 9th fret and strum)

Well, if I get my hands on a dol-lar bill, gon-na buy a bot-tle and drink my fill. If I get my hands on a num-ber five, gon-na *skin that little girl alive. If I get my hands on a number two come back home and marry you, marry you, marry you. All right!*

Land _____ Ho!

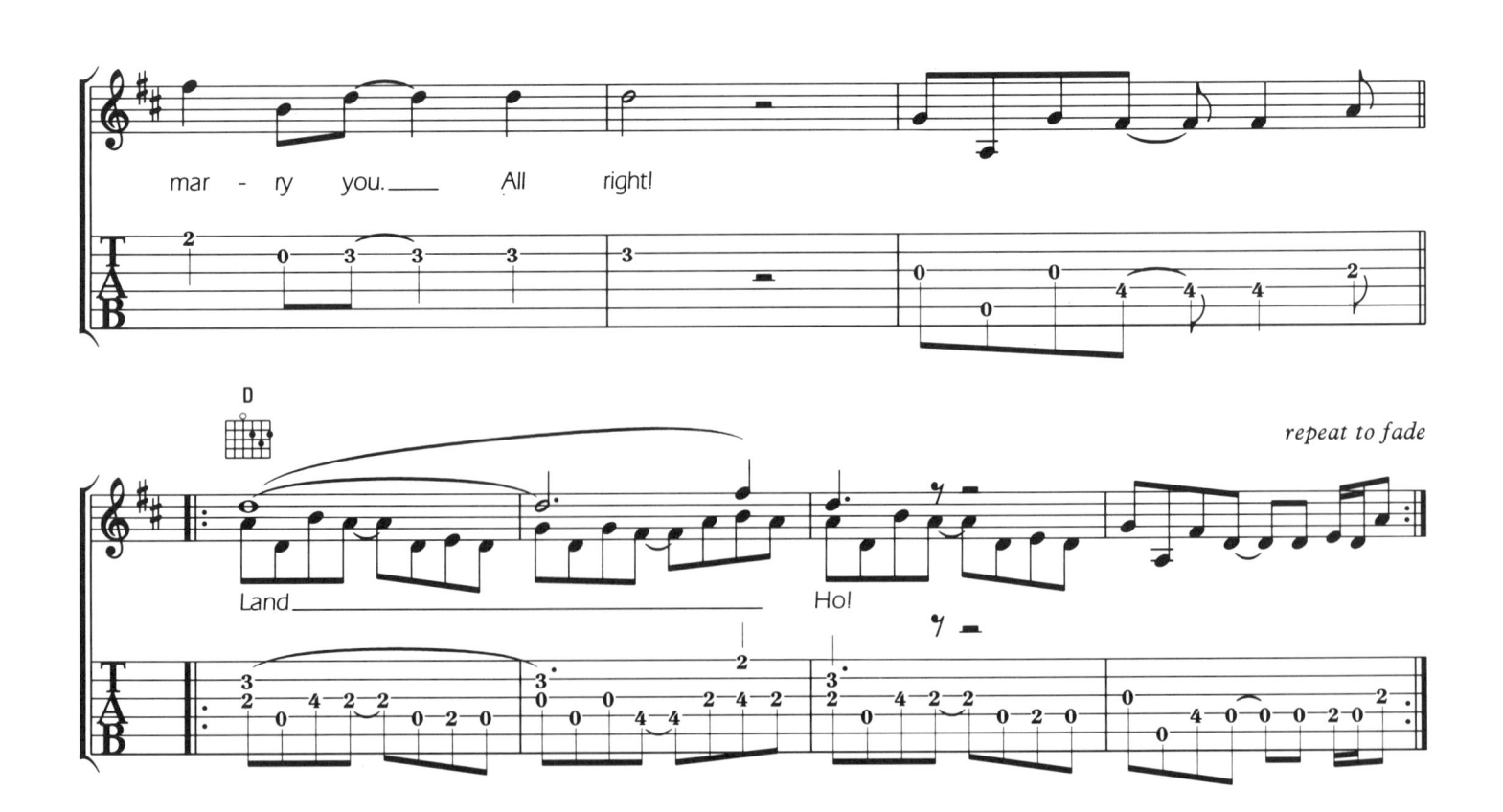

repeat to fade

2. This old man was graceful, with silver in his smile.
   He smoked a briar pipe and he walked four country miles.
   Singing songs of shady sisters and old time liberty,
   Songs of love and songs of death, and song to set men free.
   Stand at mast, let north winds blow till half of us are dead.
   Land Ho!

THE END

Words & Music by The Doors

© Copyright 1967 Doors Music Company, USA. All rights for the United
Kingdom, Northern Ireland & Eire controlled by Rondor Music (London)
Limited, 10a Parsons Green, London SW6.
All Rights Reserved. International Copyright Secured.

Sixth String to D

This is the end, beau-ti-ful friend.

This is the end, my on-ly friend, the end of our e-lab-orate

plans, the end of ev-ery-thing that stands, the end, No

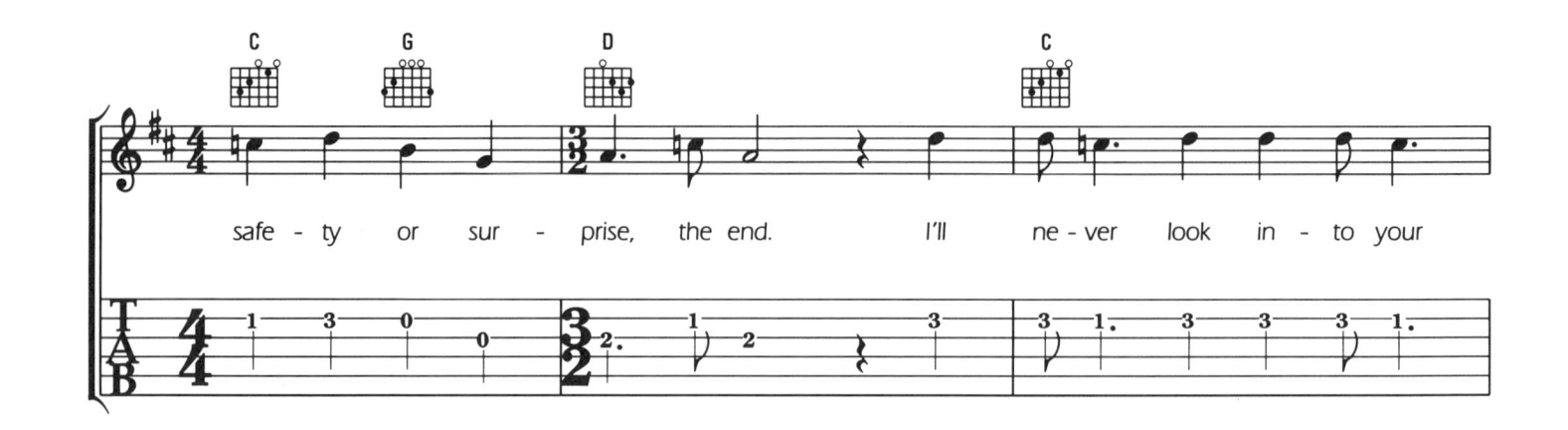

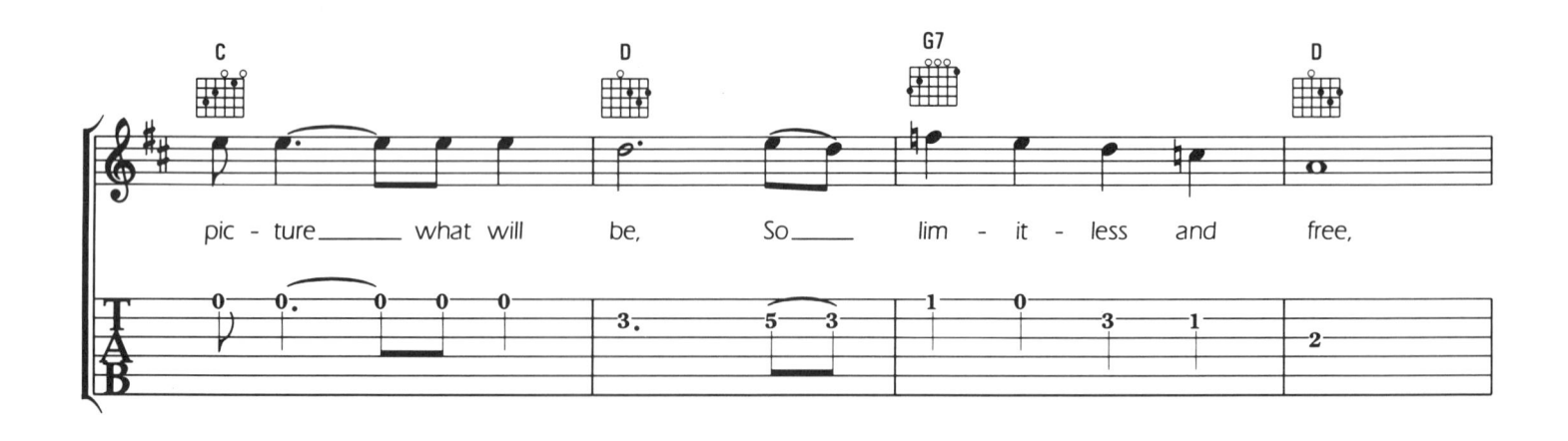

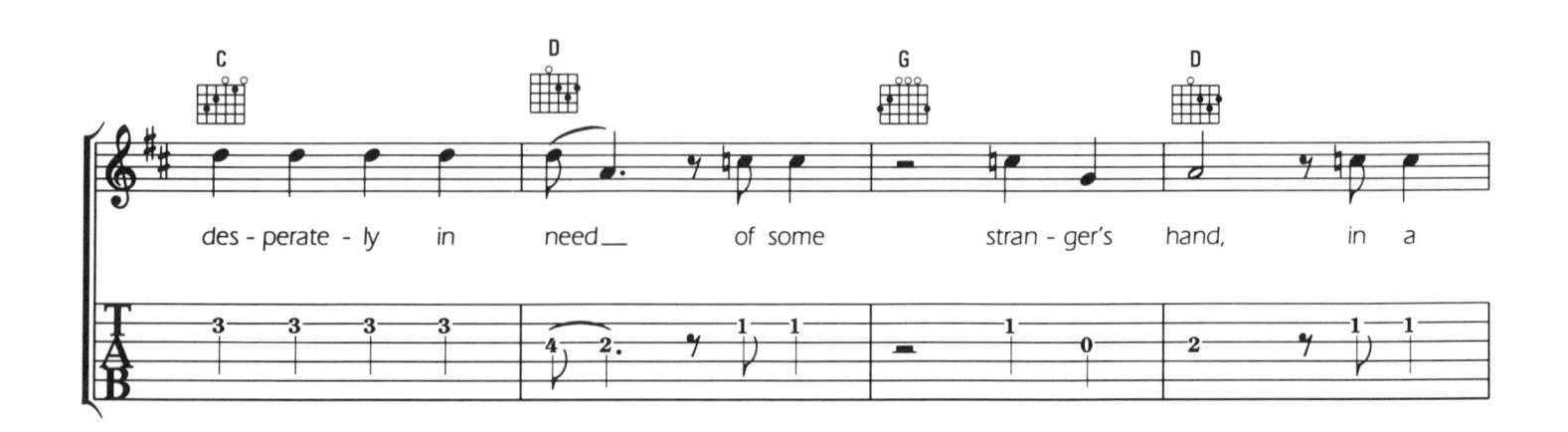

safe - ty or sur - prise, the end. I'll ne - ver look in - to your eyes a - gain. Can you pic - ture what will be, So lim - it - less and free, des - per - ate - ly in need of some stran - ger's hand, in a des - perate land.

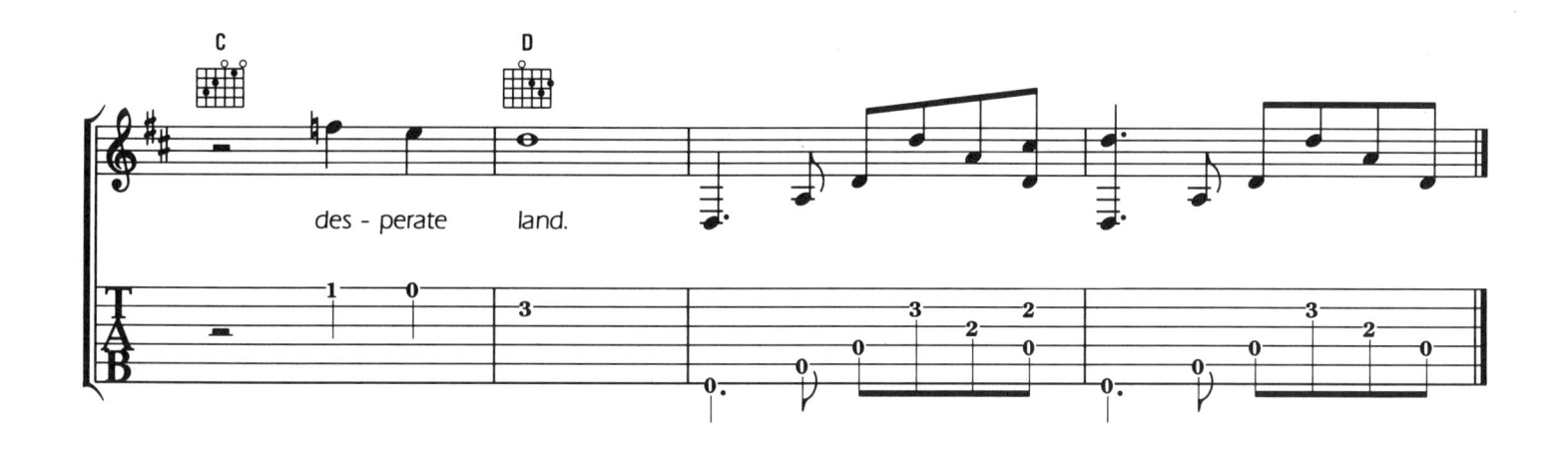

Lost in a Roman wilderness of pain,
And all the children are insane;
All the children are insane;
Waiting for the summer rain.

There's danger on the edge of town,
Ride the King's highway.
Wierd scenes inside the goldmine;
Ride the King's highway west, baby.

Ride the snake, to the lake, The ancient lake.
The snake is long, seven miles;
Ride the snake, He's best.
The west is the best.
Get here and we'll do the rest.

The blue bus is calling us.
Driver, where you taking us?

The killer awoke before dawn,
He put his boots on,
He took a face from the ancient gallery,
And he walked on down the hall.

He went to the room where his sister lived,
And then he pais a visit to his brother,
And then he walked on down the hall.

And then he came to a door,
And he looked inside,
'Father?'
'Yes, son?'
'I want to kill you.'
'Mother, I want to ...'

It hurts to set you free but you'll never follow me.
Come on, baby, take a chance with us,
And meet me at the back of the blue bus.

ALABAMA SONG

Music by Kurt Weill. Words by Bertolt Brecht.

© Copyright 1929 by Universal Edition. Copyright renewed 1956 by Mrs. Karoline Weill-Davis,
New York for the USA. Copyright for all other countries Universal Edition A.G. Wien.
All Rights Reserved. International Copyright Secured.

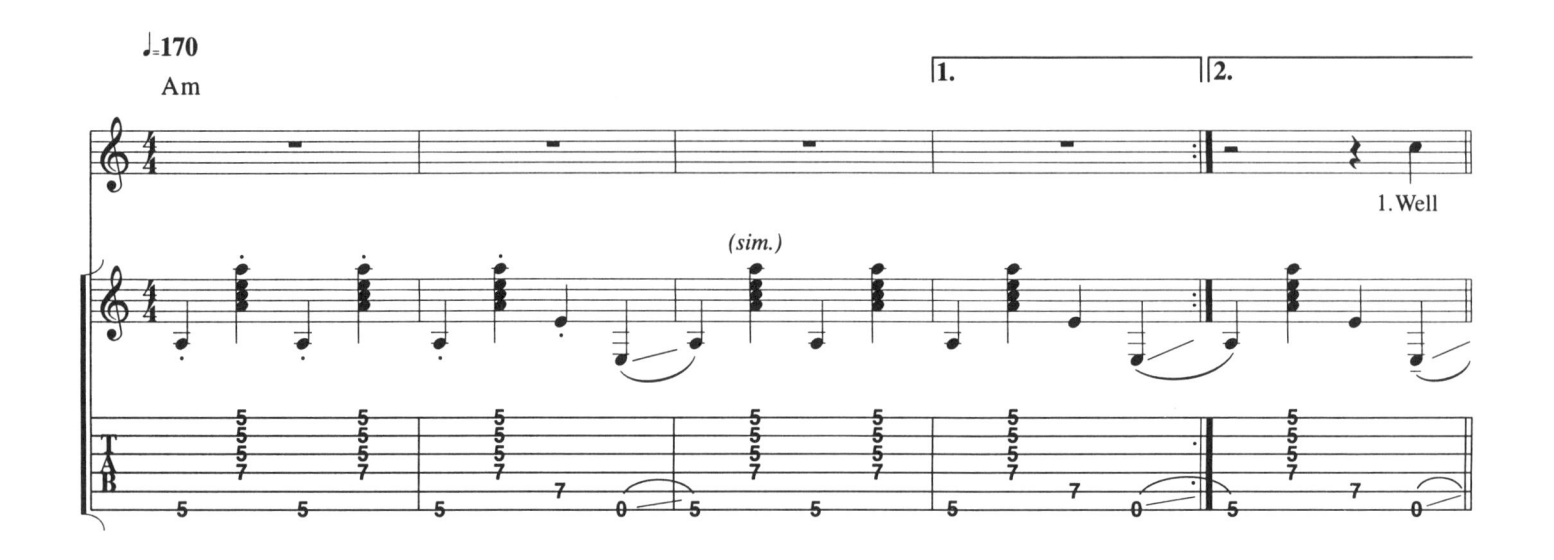

Verses 1 & 2

show me the way to the next whisky bar, oh, don't ask why,
See additional lyrics for verse 2

oh, don't ask why. Show me the way to the next whisky bar,

* On 𝄋 the first 4 bars of verse 2 are A major

oh, don't ask why, oh, don't ask why. For if (a)-we don't find the next whis-ky bar I tell you we must die, I tell you we must die, I tell you, I tell you, I tell you we must die.

Chorus
Oh, moon of A-la-ba-ma, and

hold............. sim.
on %. instrumental for 16 bars

now must say good-bye,_____ we've_ lost our good old_____ ma-ma and must have whis-key oh_ you know why._____ Oh, moon of A-la-ba-----ma, and now must say good-bye._____ We've_ lost our good old

Verse 2 (𝄋):
Well show me the way to the next little girl
Oh, don't ask why, oh don't ask why
Show me the way to the next little girl
Oh, don't ask why, oh don't ask why.
For if we don't find the next little girl
I tell you we must die, I tell you we must die
I tell you, I tell you
I tell you we must die.

BACK DOOR MAN

Words & Music by Willie Dixon.

© Copyright Hoochie Coochie Music, USA,
administered by Bug Music Limited, 75 Milson Road, London W14.
All Rights Reserved. International Copyright Secured.

this bend and similar bends are flat throughout

(+ organ)

Oh, yeah—

%　Verses 1, 2 & 3

I'm a—　I'm a back door man,—

See additional lyrics for verses 2 & 3

D7
A7
I'm a back door man, the
hold
½
¼
E7
D7
To Coda
A
1.
men don't know, but the lit-tle girls un-der-stand.
hold
½
P.M.
(sim.)
2.
A7
Solo
f
P.M.
1
D7
A7
rake
½

54

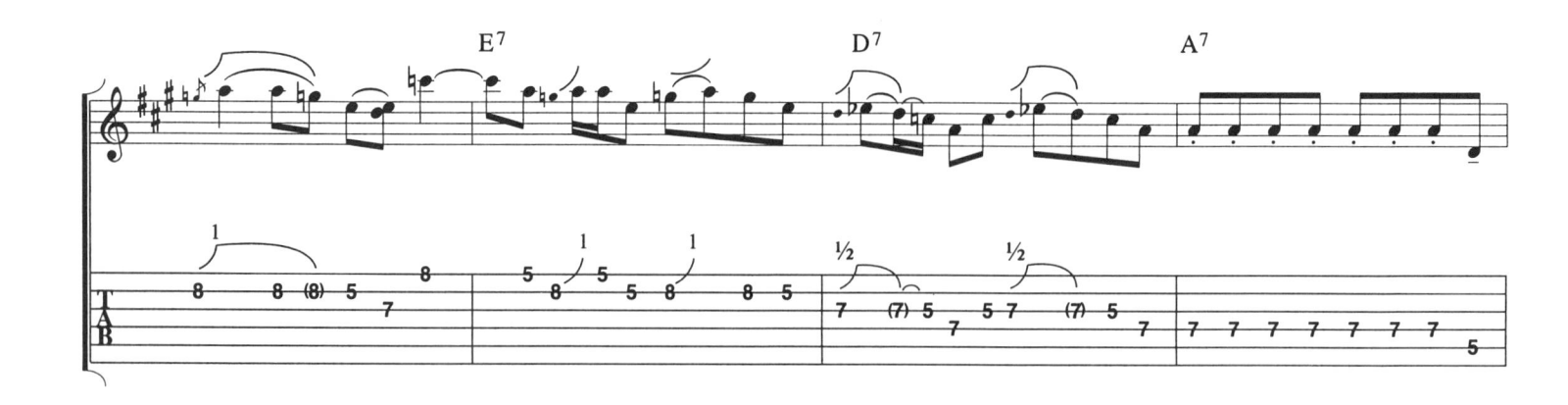

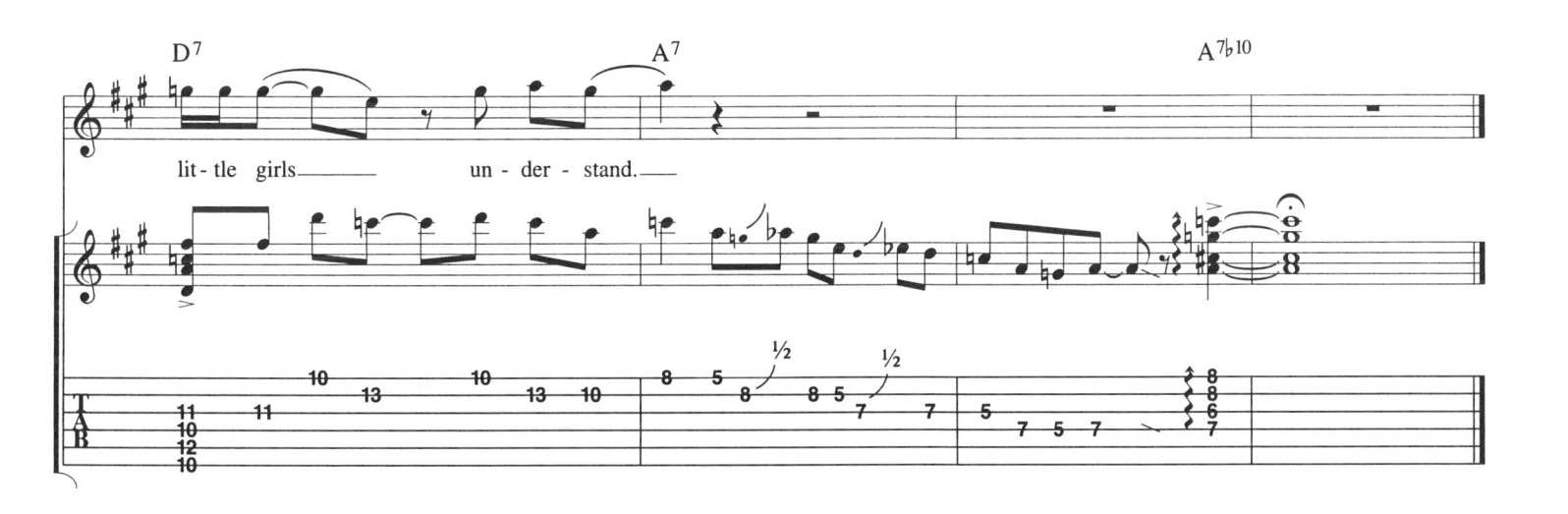

Verse 2:
Hey all you people there tryin' to sleep
I'm out to make it with my midnight treat
Yeah, took down the back door man
The men don't know but the little girls understand.

Verse 3 (𝄋):
You men eat your dinner, eat your poor canned beans
I eat more chicken than a man ever seen, yeah, yeah
I'm a back door man
The men don't know but the little girls understand.

Bringing you the words

All the latest in rock and pop. Plus the brightest and best in West End show scores. Music books for every instrument under the sun. And exciting new teach-yourself ideas like "Let's Play Keyboard" - in cassette/book packs, or on video. Available from all good music shops.

and music

Music Sales' complete catalogue lists thousands of titles and is available free from your local music shop, or direct from Music Sales Limited. Please send a cheque or postal order for £1.50 (for postage) to:

Music Sales Limited
Newmarket Road,
Bury St Edmunds,
Suffolk IP33 3YB

Bringing you the world's best music.